The Parent's Book of
BALLET

*Answers to critical questions
about the care and development
of the young dancer*

By
ANGELA WHITEHILL
and
WILLIAM NOBLE

MERIWETHER PUBLISHING LTD.
COLORADO SPRINGS, COLORADO

Meriwether Publishing Ltd., Publisher
P.O. Box 7710
Colorado Springs, CO 80933

Editor: Arthur Zapel
Typesetting: Sharon Garlock
Design and illustration: Michelle Gallardo
Cover photography: *(top photo)* **Jack Mitchel**
 (bottom photo and backcover photo) **Ted Zapel**
Cover dancers: *(top photo)* **Lauren E. Gelfand in the Boston Ballet's**
 A Midsummer Night's Dream
 (bottom photo) **Jennifer Shrewsbury and Leanne Schreiner,**
 courtesy of Esther Geoffrey, Colorado College Ballet Studio.
 (back cover) **Jennifer Shrewsbury and Jennifer Stone, courtesy**
 of Esther Geoffery, Colorado College Ballet Studio.

Library of Congress Cataloging-in-Publication Data

Whitehill, Angela, 1938-
 The parents book of ballet.

 Bibliography: p.
 1. Ballet—Study and teaching. I. Noble, William.
II. Title.
GV1788.5.W48   1988   792.8'2   88-13658
ISBN 0-916260-52-6

For Audrey and
in memory of Paul

CONTENTS

FOREWORD 1

Part I:
The Beginning Years *(ages 4-7)* 5
    Chapter 1: The Best Age to Begin Ballet 7
    Chapter 2: Pre-Ballet Classes 13
    Chapter 3: Finding the Right Teacher 19
    Chapter 4: Ballet Outside the Studio 25

Part II:
The Recital Trap 31

Part III:
The Pre-teen Years *(ages 8-12)* 39
    Chapter 1: Learning the Childrens' Ballet Syllabus 41
    Chapter 2: Going "on pointe" — How and Why 47
    Chapter 3: All about Pointe Shoes 53
    Chapter 4: The Ballet Body 61
    Chapter 5: Special Training for Boys 69

Part IV:
Auditions for the Young Dancer 73

Part V:
The Early Teen Years *(ages 13-15)* 85
    Chapter 1: Lifestyle of the Teenaged Dancer 87
    Chapter 2: Performing Arts Schools 93
    Chapter 3: Proper Weight and Improper Habits 101
    Chapter 4: The Regional Ballet Experience 109
    Chapter 5: Jazz and Modern Dancing 117

Part VI:
Summer Programs 125

Part VIII:
The Later Years *(ages 16-18)* 137
    Chapter 1: College Dance Alternative 139
    Chapter 2: A Full Time Dance Career Now? 147

AFTERWORD — *What Next?* 153
APPENDIX 157
GLOSSARY 173
BIBLIOGRAPHY 179
ABOUT THE AUTHORS 181
PHOTO CREDITS 183

Master teacher David Howard teaching Jennifer Gelfand.

FOREWORD
by
David Howard

"My fourteen-year-old daughter attends a performing arts high school..." begins a letter from the father of a young ballet dancer. "I feel she should be in a higher level, but her teacher doesn't think so ... I would like your advice on what I should do..."

I receive letters like this month after month, year after year, all of them seeking help so their talented children can take full advantge of a possible ballet career. As teacher and director I understand the many questions parents and their young dancers have, and through the years I have tried to be as honest and helpful as I could. I well remember my own early training in England, and the bouts of confusion and uncertainty that buffetted me. Ballet training is complicated, frustrating and extremely difficult. All young dancers and their parents would not be normal if they didn't have a box full of questions for their teachers.

The real issue, however, is whether there might be answers to these questions. Ballet is an art form with a split personality — the demands on our bodies, the preciseness of the steps we perform require discipline and order; yet our training of young dancers varies from school to school (mine, for example, applies principles of kinesiology to the steps of dance movement and combines it all with innate musicality — others have different procedures).

We who do the training know the answers to the questions parents put forward. But it simply doesn't occur to us that parents and their young dancers might be shy about seeking seemingly simple information such as how do I find a good teacher, or do boys have different training than girls? Sometimes parents aren't quite sure precisely what information they want, only that they feel a lack of hard facts, and they sense some uncertainty.

In a sense it is a communications gap, and we, as teachers of young dancers, must take the first step toward closing it. Our responsibilities with our students require nothing less, and that is

1

why this book is both timely and valuable. It fills a need. Parents, teachers, young dancers, even the audience, will find resources not previously set out in such great detail, and some of the mystery of the ballet training process will be opened up for all to see.

The process of creating a ballet dancer has been shrouded in mystery through the decades. Questions about training, auditions, schools, summer programs, had no central answering service. The best authority was usually a teacher or an active artistic director. But no one could answer for the others, and the result was a hodgepodge of information that combined personal experience with personal bias and provided no unvarying standard. For a parent or a young dancer seeking only one simple, sure answer, it was confusing, to say the least.

This book finally puts things in order, and it explains in clear words the pros and the cons of the ballet process. In my opinion, choices and timing are of the utmost importance in a dancer's career. Where to study, whether and when to attend a boarding school, how to find the right teacher, when to go on pointe, are the kinds of serious questions all parents should ask because the answers are often complex. The authors of this book take the time to show the proper way to approach such matters.

In the past twenty years ballet has spread itself more thoroughly across the face of America, and the result has been greater ballet interest in city after city. I see it in my studio where students are coming in with stronger training and background from hundreds, even thousands, of miles away. Dance has become decentralized, and this pleases me greatly because ballet is an art form for all, not just for the sophisticated few. *The Parents Book of Ballet* recognizes this by offering insights from artistic directors throughout the country and by highlighting the regional ballet experience. Ballet is no longer synonymous with New York City even though many young dancers continue to see themselves only on stage with Joffrey Ballet, American Ballet Theatre or the New York City Ballet. These companies, however, can accommodate but 300 to 400 dancers, and those aspiring to such places number in the many thousands. This book emphasizes that there are other excellent options available, that dancers can find a happy quality of life elsewhere, that there are fine ballet companies in such places as Atlanta, Pittsburgh, Dayton, Des Moines and Seattle.

If there is one thing I feel strongly about it is that the early development of the dancer is vitally important. Without this early training no dancer can feel the true flow of movement so necessary later on. This book will help guide parents through the joys of a classical training and prepare the young dancer to make the ultimate choice about a career. Every responsible teacher should have a copy in their studio and make it available not only to aspiring dancers, but to their parents as well. Finally, I think, those questions parents and their young dancers ask now have answers we can all support.

DAVID HOWARD

David Howard students can be easily recognized on the stages of ballet companies great and small, in modern dance companies and on Broadway, television and motion pictures. A teacher of unique ability, his principles of dance instruction have kept him in constant demand internationally. He has been a ballet teacher in Europe and the U.S. with students of renown including: Mikhail Baryshnikov, Patrick Dupond, Sylvia Guillem, Jennifer Gelfand, Alesandra Ferri and Rudolph Nureyev. Currently, he is the director of the David Howard Dance Center in New York City.

Part I:

The Beginning Years

(ages 4-7)

Creative dance introduces the young child to the discipline of the art.

---Chapter 1:---

The Best Age to Begin Ballet

Every August the studio phone starts to ring; it's the beginning of another season, another ballet school semester. Parents are calling to enroll their children in class, and with the certainty of the season comes the frequent question:

"What age do you start children's ballet classes?"

The answer never varies. "Five years old for pre-ballet, seven or eight years old for regular ballet."

Sometimes there is a hush of disappointment. "My child is almost four, but she has a lovely little body. She's been dancing since she could walk..."

"She's too young, right now."

The parent is undeterred. "She used to point her toes in the crib. Every time we play music she gets up and dances. She moves her arms so gracefully. She's beautiful..."

Three years old, even four years old is simply too young to begin to learn the rudiments of ballet, and any reasonably good ballet teacher will agree. Yet the demand for dance classes, even for the youngest age, has become so great that most ballet schools offer something they call "creative dance" — a preliminary type of instruction that touches on dance and music appreciation but does not include any formal ballet training.

"We begin our creative dance classes with three-and- one-half to four year olds," says Anne Marie Rebassi, an instructor with the Central Pennsylvania Youth Ballet. "At that age the children have an extremely limited attention span, so we keep the classes to a half hour, and we make no attempt to introduce ballet steps or terminology."

The children are shown various forms of shape and movement, items they easily recognize, such as a butterfly, a bubble, a flower, a cat or pony. Then they learn to beat out the syllables of their names on the floor with their hands and/or feet in a rhythmic pattern. They make shapes with their bodies — such as the letter "C" by curving their backs, or a diamond by bending their legs outward — and they act out simple stories and nursery rhymes. The point is to get them used to using their bodies in order to say something.

"I can't wait to see my little one in a tutu," the parent will often exclaim.

It will be a long wait. Occasionally, in the creative dance classes, the students may be allowed to dress up in an old costume or wear a tiara. But tutus? "This isn't a ballet class," says Rebassi. "I try to teach them some classroom etiquette — how to listen and follow, not to talk — and I show them that there are different kinds of music."

And that's all she does.

Of course, there are times when parents and children are their own worst enemies...

At the age of three my mother took me to my first dance class. She had dreamed of becoming a dancer but due to a family disaster, she had stopped taking classes at an early age. Now, as with so many women when they become mothers, she wanted all for me she never had. I remember the beautiful stairway that curved gracefully to the second floor studio, and I remember being filled with excitement. My mother guided me into the dressing room where the girls changed into little blue tunics and the boys into shorts. We were ushered into a huge white and gold room with two bay windows and a beautiful, shining wood floor.

First, we sat on the floor and wiggled our toes;

then we flexed our feet and hands; then we were told to stand.

"Now we will run around and shoot our bows," said Miss Cookearborough, the teacher.

Oh no, I remember thinking. I came to be a ballerina, not to shoot things! I stood absolutely still, and ten little children piled into me, knocking us all to the floor. I burst into tears and refused to move.

Miss Cookearborough took in the scene quickly and invited my mother to join the class instead. I was picked up and set in the window seat to watch.

This went on for three weeks. By now my mother had learned all that a three-year-old could be taught, and we left the class permanently.

I didn't return to dance until I was ten years old — after seeing a performance of the Metropolitan Ballet with Celia Franca, who subsequently became my teacher in Canada...

Because the very young child constitutes a large part of the studio income, sometimes it is hard for a teacher to refuse them admission, especially in small towns where the overall number of students may not be high. But the first step should be the creative dance experience, and from that the ballet end product will be more satisfying.

Unfortunately, there are parents of three- and four-year-olds who won't be deterred by a refusal to teach their little ones formal ballet. If they try hard enough, they will probably find someone who will take their child, but the consequences can be enormous. The child may be taught incorrectly or may be hurt because of the physical demands or may simply become bored... and the dream of a ballet career could be over before it really begins.

A proper dance instruction is based on the child's physical ability and stage of development. At four years old a youngster's bones are quite soft and malleable, and severe damage could result from overly arduous training or exertion. Even the best and most caring teacher is not equipped to pinpoint a child's level of development at this young age — only a pediatrician could know for certain. The good ballet teacher will explain these risks to a parent adamant enough to want pure ballet training for a four-year-old. The creative dance experience can be fun for the little one, and its de-

9

mands won't be overly taxing.

Sometimes, however, there are children at the age of four who are so determined to dance and have made up their minds that there's little use in trying to deter them. A few, indeed, even go on to have successful careers, though many do become burned out. But if a child like this is in the house, what can be done?

First, call the largest dance schools in the area and ask them about their teaching philosophies: do they follow a graded system; do they have recitals (see Part 2); how many children in a class; have they had any students join professional companies; at what age do the students go "on pointe" (if before nine years old, don't even consider — see Part 3)?

Next, ask to come in and watch a class of four-year-olds and a class of six- to seven-year-olds. See how much repetition of content there is in each class; if it exists, the chances are any new student will be subjected to the same thing, and this could go on for up to four years — or until the child is eight or nine. Quite a boring prospect. Children don't want to be flowers, trees or kittens for that long, they want variety.

Then, check and see if the same teacher is teaching all the classes. This, too, can become boring for a little one.

Does the school offer a recital? We'll see more on that later

Four and five year olds learn various shapes and movement.

on, but most classical ballet teachers believe that four years old is too young to take the pressure of a recital. Talk to the parents in both classes, ask how their children have reacted, then talk to the teacher and see if she really understands the tiny child. Ask how much she expects of the creative dance class, and if she expects the students to learn technique such as barre work, arabesques and pirouettes. If so, be very cautious.

But when the child becomes five years old, another level is reached. Now pre-ballet classes are appropriate and here the children get their first exposure to formal ballet. There are, in fact, some well recognized teachers who believe no child should even enter a dance class before the age of five. Pre-ballet should be the first group dance exposure, and the reasoning is simply that before the age of five, little that is taught will be retained, and a later start can only be of ultimate benefit.

But the creative dance experience should not be worthless, providing no one expects too much, and little, if any, performing pressure is placed on the child. The time for all that pressure and performing will come later on.

The key is this: there are reasons why a child should start dance training at a particular age, and just because the little moppet looks so cute in a pale pink tutu when grandmother comes to visit doesn't mean she or he is ready to begin formal ballet training.

Beginning students must learn simple ports de bras (arm movements and positions).

Chapter 2:
Pre-Ballet Classes

A year can make such a difference! Five-year-olds with a season of creative dance behind them will quickly appreciate that such creative expression is to be channeled to rigid standards, that what was applauded as a four-year-old's sense of imagination will now become a five-year-old's lack of discipline.

It is the first lesson on the front edge of a possible ballet career. Ballet is discipline, it is a close following of prescribed movements, it is strange and it is exciting.

The class opens... "Face the barre," the teacher says, pointing to the rounded wood or metal shape attached to the wall and running parallel to the floor. "Now put both your hands on it ... gently, gently ..."

The little ones are thrilled, until now they haven't been allowed to touch the barre. First, the teacher shows them two of the five ballet feet positions (the other three foot positions are more complicated and should not be attempted until the children are at least eight years old), and she explains that these should be done with a forty-five degree "turn out".

To five-year-olds this means nothing, other than their first exposure to a new ballet term. But they watch as she rotates her

Foot Positions

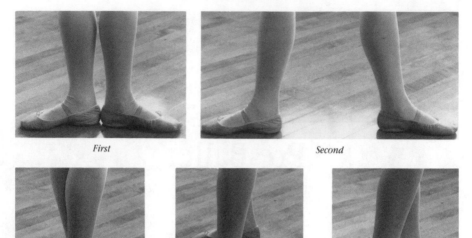

First

Second

Third

Fourth

Fifth

entire leg with the knee, calf, ankle and foot in strict alignment and at a forty-five degree angle to the perpendicular of her body.

"We use turn out to make it easier to move in all directions," she says, pointing to her hip and emphasizing that everything begins from there. "Try it," she encourages, and little legs fly out unceremoniously.

Slowly, the teacher will explain a few basic warm-up exercises, showing them how they must learn to bend. "We're trying to find our balance," she adds, and the little bodies try a variety of positions. She has them watch her as she slowly sinks in a small half-knee bend. "We call this a 'demi-plie'," she says. "See how the legs turn out. We are making a diamond shape."

As they try to follow her, she watches them carefully. It is the first ballet exercise they will encounter, and she wants to make sure that, as they turn out, their little knees will travel sideways and hold directly over the middle toe of the foot.

This is the only proper way to do a 'demi-plie'. "Let's do some stretching," the teacher says. "Shall we be mice or snails?" The children remember that these are the exercises they learned in creative dance the year before. What they don't realize is that this role playing is essential to all dance performance.

"Now let's try first position as we gallop across the floor..."

"Here's how we jump in first position..."

Little bodies in motion bobbing like heated popcorn...

The teacher relaxes and smiles at her class. The forty-five minute time has sped by, and the five-year-olds are filled with excitement and curiosity. It is more than enough for one day.

But without realizing it the little ones have experienced the basic structure of a classical ballet class. It will not vary, no matter their age, no matter their level of accomplishment, professional dancer or limited amateur. The first pre-ballet class has established the pattern.

The idea of pre-ballet classes isn't without its critics. Anne Marie Rebassi is one of these. "I don't really like to have kids under the age of seven," she says, "because they are still growing physically. At seven or eight their minds and bodies begin to mesh, and this makes learning and teaching so much easier." Madeline Cantrella Culpo, artistic director of the Berkshire Ballet Theatre in Pittsfield, Massachusetts, agrees. She thinks children are starting too young. "But do you have a choice?" she asks, admitting that non-ballet dance forms such as jazz and tap will be happy to take the young child if ballet won't. "I do give pre-ballet lessons at four, but I find that four-year-olds today are more sophisticated than they were twenty years ago."

The children may enter their pre-ballet classes at a young age, but that doesn't mean they will progress quicker. "I tell every mother," Madeline Culpo says, "that I will not put her child into classical ballet classes until the child is seven. They must know the pre-ballet experience could last for up to three years."

Beyond the actual ballet steps, what can the child learn in the pre-ballet years? At five and six, a child has an innocent facility to accept and remember words, names and phrases in another language, and of course the language of ballet is French. Most little ones pick up the terminology as easily as they would learn English equivalents. At this time, too, the children are beginning to understand and feel their bodies, and they are responsive to simple correction; they *want* to learn. This is also a good time to introduce music, and to teach the child to listen and HEAR tempos and rhythms. Familiarity with all of this will bridge an important gap when formal ballet classes begin.

Posture is an extremely important part of the pre-ballet class. The five/six-year-old is only beginning to lose "baby fat" as well as his or her round little tummy, and this is the best time to teach the proper position. Correct ballet posture involves the body held slightly forward over the front third of the foot, the knees held over the toes and with the backs of the knees pulled up, the thighs should be rotated so that the inner thigh can be seen. The lower abdominal muscles should be pulled up, the rib cage lifted but not distended, shoulders relaxed naturally, neck gracefully stretched, and the head held erect, not protruding forward.

Then ... the upper back will be held straight and the buttocks controlled in such a way that the spine will look like a straight line from the nape of the neck to the tail bone.

The correct ballet posture — not simple, not without arduous training, but it can be learned in pre-ballet class.

A note of caution. Many children show an interest in gymnastics at this age, and it might seem as if ballet and gymnastics would complement one another well. Not true. Ballet can help gymnastics, especially for floor exercises, but the ballet dancer needs to maintain a straight spine. This is where the two disciplines diverge: gymnastics requires the student to curve the lower back when landing, and the ballet dancer must have that strong, *straight* back.

Anything less than that and the ballet dancer might as well kiss away a professional career.

As the pre-ballet classes move along, the children will be taught a variety of ballet steps: relevés, battement tendu, piqúe, retiré or passé, and the preparation for grand battement. All these exercises start and finish in first position, the easiest and most familiar position for the feet to assume, and dancers — even in pre-ballet class — who can combine an understanding of these steps with the proper posture are well on their way to ballet success.

But let's not forget the arms. Ballet involves the total body, and the way the arms perform is equally as important as how the legs are seen. Pre-ballet classes get to work on the arms, too.

There are five basic arm positions, all based on a circle, each position held in front of the shoulders. Sometimes they are introduced with games and imagery, making it more fun for the little ones. "I take a poem," says Anne Marie Rebassi, "and I have the children use their bodies, their arms and imagine the poem through dance." She has them move their arms in order to illustrate the poem physically, and she encourages them to *feel* the words.

As the class progresses, it's obvious the children are getting restless. Too much stationary work can be boring, especially to a five year old.

"Let's move over to the corner," says the teacher, and she directs them to execute some traveling steps, moving diagonally across the room. "Try to gallop, like a horse," she says. "Go forward ... now sideways ... now back ..." Then she pairs them up, and has them make simple skips with the toe lifted to the knee, moving together, seeking a rhythm.

"Pretend there's a pool of water in the middle of the room," she says. "Let's jump over it ..." And she has them imitate a horse, up and over, legs extended, if possible.

The tiniest preparation for the big jumps that every ballet dancer must execute in the years ahead.

Then the class is over. And the teacher nods at her students. In unison the five-year-olds curtsy or bow, and the teacher smiles.

No ballet class is complete without this curtsy or bow. Ballet is an extremely polite art, and it has a specific etiquette. To curtsy or bow is to say thank you and to show appreciation.

The teacher is content. It has been a good class.

Finding the right teacher takes care and research.

Chapter 3

Finding the Right Teacher

The art of ballet is a multiple discipline, combining a varied assortment of dance, movement and music with an appreciation of painting, literature, history and sculpture. It is not enough to teach a series of steps and sit back contentedly while the student tries to make sense of what has been taught.

The fine ballet teacher is an artist *first* — then a teacher. Not the other way around.

The fine ballet teacher infuses a child with a deep love of all the arts, and to do this the teacher must have a personal respect and love for the ballet art form. The teacher must believe in it, and must live it.

Parents must search out the teacher's background, and the key is to determine if the teacher has a minimum of six to ten years of training with a recognized and reliable ballet school such as Virginia Intermont College, School of American Ballet, San Francisco Ballet, Hartford Ballet or a school attached to a professional company either in the United States or abroad. While professional stage experience is not mandatory, it is certainly helpful. But note this: *There are many fine teachers who have not danced professionally; a teacher with careful training and no professional experi-*

ence is far preferable to one with poor training and extensive stage experience.

What if the teacher teaches many dance forms (such as jazz, modern *and* ballet)? Be careful here. Most highly qualified ballet teachers limit themselves to ballet only. If the studio offers other dance forms, be sure other qualified teachers will teach them. The ballet art form is too highly specialized and too demanding for a teacher to taint her ballet discipline with other dance techniques. Good ballet teachers just don't spread themselves into other dance forms.

An important consideration must be the instructional syllabus that the teacher and the school will follow, and parents should become familiar with the overall plan. There are a number of recognized syllabuses, all based on Russian, French, English, Danish or Italian ballet traditions, and any one of them would be appropriate for a child. The syllabus is the actual plan of instruction — the number of classes per day and week, the movements to be learned and followed, body emphasis (in Russia, for example, the system trains particularly strong and muscular dancers) and the yearly progression of skills. The syllabus should take the child from the point of entry into the ballet world to the pre-professional level, a period of at least eight years.

Classical ballet was formalized by Louis XIV of France who created the Academie de Danse in 1631 in Paris, and because of this all ballet terms have remained French. But the art developed in other European countries and with it certain definable ballet traditions. For example, in Italy, Enrico Cecchetti created a beautiful system which emphasizes the ports de bras (carriage of the arms and body), while in England, Adeline Gennée created the Royal Academy of Dancing which established an exacting grade system for dancers starting at age eight and running to age eighteen.

The point is that while these and the other recognized European systems are taught in the United States, they are excellent instructional plans, reliable and substantial. In particular, the Cecchetti and Royal Academy of Dancing systems offer yearly refresher courses for teachers and examinations for students. Because of their wide acceptance, the examination results for students from both systems can be evaluated on a national and an international level.

What, then, might an appropriate examination syllabus contain? It will include barre and centre work, a simple dance and in some cases mime and character dancing. Because there is "preset" work, some of the examination preparation time can become a bit tedious, and a truly talented ballet teacher will prepare her students with a mixture of syllabus work *and* other aspects of technique, including — in the higher grades — some performance and repertoire.

But the syllabus is the key to everything. Some fine teachers do not wish to adhere to the rigid demands of a pre-conceived syllabus, preferring instead to follow their own designs. There is nothing wrong with this provided they have a sound knowledge of the existing systems (including the Vaganova system from Russia, the Bournonville system from Denmark, as well as the Cecchetti and Royal Academy of Dancing systems), and they provide a sound grading system. In some cases, this can have a happy effect on the child because the teacher represents a varied learning history that comprises the best of everything.

The important thing to remember . . . ask! Find out the syllabus the teacher and the studio follow. Make sure it is firmly based on the European tradition.

A major consideration is when the children are allowed to begin dancing "on pointe". Any school that starts them before the age of nine or ten should *not* be considered.

The teacher should give verbal and "hands on" correction.

Why? It's a case of the willing mind and the unwilling body. Children may "think" they are ready to go on pointe, but a young child's bones are soft and malleable before nine or ten, and long-lasting damage can occur in the legs and back if the body isn't ready for the heavy pointe demands. The first two or three years of syllabus work are carefully designed to teach the child the correct use of the muscles which will eventually be used for dancing on the toes.

There are, of course, exceptional children who can start this training early. But these are few in number, and most good ballet teachers carry a built-in skepticism about such things. Six-year-olds, seven-year-olds are too young! Period!

Once in a while, though . . . Cherie Noble became a member of the Pennsylvania Ballet Company at fourteen, and ten years earlier — at the age of four — she started her formal ballet training. By the time she was six she was given pointe shoes because "I insisted on running all over the house and studio on full pointe," she laughs, "without shoes! They gave me pointe shoes so I wouldn't hurt myself."

Later, she became ballet mistress of the Pennsylvania Ballet and a well-recognized master teacher at numerous other companies and schools. Her feet remain as sturdy as ever. Occasionally in class, she will remove her flat ballet shoes, and barefoot, rise to her toes and hold the pointe position.

But she is the exception, the *real* exception.

Unfortunately, there is no licensing requirement for dance teachers, and while the profession has tried self-policing, it has met with indifferent results. There are some dance teacher organizations that examine teachers for membership, but they are not geared especially for ballet.

The best way to choose a teacher and a school is to ask questions and to follow the steps outlined. Visit the school and watch a class. The teacher should be giving verbal and "hands on" corrections; it should be a disciplined class. Do not — repeat, do not! — choose a teacher because of location, price or convenience. Ease of car pooling, allowing a child to be with her best friend a couple of hours more each day, are *not* reasons to choose either a teacher or a school. Improper training can result in malformed bones, improper muscle structure and career frustration. Ballet training is serious training, and it should be approached in a serious manner.

Is there a right teacher for everyone?

Absolutely.

Finding that teacher isn't hard if we know where to look and what to look for:

— an artist, *first*
— strong training fundamentals
— well-disciplined approach to students
— carefully designed syllabus of instruction

The right teacher.

Reading books about ballet helps the child understand the art form.

————Chapter 4:————

Ballet Outside
the Studio

"You could tell that ballet was her life," says a principal
dancer with the New York City Ballet, referring to Alexandra
Danilova, and remembering that always Madame came to class in
a matching outfit and perfume. "She was so feminine..."

Ballet was her life!

Her central motivator, her consuming passion, it meant
that the extraneous pieces of her existence could come together
when ballet was involved. Her life and her art became one.

Ballet is not a dance discipline that should be left within
the walls of the studio. It needs expression in the steps of our
daily lives. The more attention it is paid here, the more creative
and effective it will be elsewhere. Ballet, to the dance professional,
is a *way* of life, and the studio is only one place where it is practiced.

Eddy Toussaint, Artistic Director of Ballet de Montreal,
says, for example, "My dancers must be princesses and princes
outside the studio as well as inside. Ballet was created for the
royal court, and it's a regal art. No chewing gum and tee shirts on
the street. Not for my dancers!"

No one expects our little ones to grapple with this level
of dedication, nor should they try to understand its effect. Yet

there is something in this portrait that should have meaning —
even for the beginning dancer.

Ballet is a *creative* art, and little ones need to be exposed
to it in its various forms, in its different manners of presentation.
Wouldn't a film, such as "The Turning Point," show an aspect of
the art that the regular Tuesday afternoon class cannot show?
Wouldn't a trip to a performing company costume shop provide
insights an hour of barre work couldn't offer?

Creativity is stimulated this way. It makes the studio work
all the more meaningful, and one never knows what will take the
beginning dancer's fantasy.

> *I took my three-year-old son to see the Pennsyl-
> vania Ballet's version of "The Nutcracker." A friend
> was dancing the Chinese variation, and she had prom-
> ised to stay in costume after the performance for my
> son. We arrived at the theatre just as the lights dimmed,
> and a white spotlight played on the conductor mount-
> ing the podium. My son's eyes grew huge as he watched
> the baton come down for the first note, and they stayed
> transfixed throughout the performance. Never once
> did he watch the dancing! Afterwards, we went back-
> stage, and my son rushed up to my friend. "Can I
> meet the 'ductor?" he asked, ignoring her elaborate
> costume. For the next year he walked around with a
> stick in his hand proclaiming his future career...*

The "Nutcracker" is probably the single most stimulating
ballet exposure any young child will get. Approximately 540 professional renditions of this beloved classic are offered in live performances throughout the United States each year, with many
ballet schools and junior ballet companies also presenting the
work. It is a Christmas pageant, and every young ballet dancer
will yearn to be a part of it.

The basic story is a fairy tale and the cast can run close
to 100 and more (see Part 5, where the full story of "The Nutcracker" is portrayed). The important thing is that the beginning
dancer can start to grasp the connection between what goes on
in the studio and how that is translated to the stage. There is
something for everyone in this ballet, from the magic of Act I, to
snow falling on stage, to sensuous Arabian dancers, to exciting
Russian folk dancing, to the Sugar Plum Fairy and her Cavalier

The "Nutcracker" is probably the first ballet a child will see.

... and finally to the sheer beauty and elegance of classical ballet. In many productions, the lead female, Clara (or Maria in some versions), and her Nutcracker Prince, fly in and out of the Kingdom of the Sweets in a balloon or ride on the back of a magic swan or in a sleigh.

The rich fantasy of "The Nutcracker" enlivens a child's sense of imagination, and this, in turn, feeds a budding creativity. But don't go to "The Nutcracker" unprepared. Read the E. T. Hoffman classic to the little one first, making sure it is one of the modern versions which relates directly to the ballet. Prepare the beginning dancer for the experience, and the results could be exciting!

But that's not all. Once a live performance of "The Nutcracker" has been seen, seek out the American Ballet Theatre's video tape of the same thing. It stars Mikhail Barishnikov and Gelsey Kirkland, and it can be played over and over. The youngster can experience the thrill of pretending she or he is on stage, understanding now that this is the ultimate goal for all ballet performers.

Books help also. The Dance Book Club, P.O. Box 57, Pennington, NJ 08534, has a regular list of titles, most of which would be useful. And in New York City, The Ballet Shop, 1887 Broadway, New York, NY 10023, around the corner from Lincoln Center, offers up-to-date material for all ages. Many books show ballet technique in words and pictures, and these can be read and explained to the beginning dancer. Among the easiest to grasp are:

1st, 2nd, 3rd and 4th Steps in Classical Ballet, by Thalia Mara, recently re-issued by Dance Horizons/ Princeton Book Company, Publishers.

The Royal Book of Ballet, by Shirley Goulden, published by Follet. This is a beautifully illustrated book, telling the stories of the most beloved ballets.

A Very Young Dancer, by Jill Krementz, published by Alfred A. Knopf. The story follows a ten-year-old girl through a season of "The Nutcracker."

How well does it work? Ask Melissa Sondrini, a principal dancer with the Hartford (Connecticut) Ballet. She's in her twenties now, but she remembers the beginning years. "When I was young, my mom kept my interest in dance through books — she never had to push me into ballet." There were other pulls on her time such as swimming and being with friends who didn't share her interest in dance. But the books were there for her to read and enjoy if she wanted . . . and there was never pressure to commit to ballet. "It was always up to me if I wanted to do one thing more than another." So she read . . . and read . . . and gradually her ballet dedication grew until she reached fifteen years of age. Then, she decided to make a career of ballet. "There was really nothing else that interested me as much as dance," she says, smiling and nodding.

For Melissa, ballet became a way of life.

Television and video tape can play an important part in enlarging the beginning dancer's dance horizons. Public televison often presents performances by some of the world's greatest ballet companies, and the little ones should be encouraged to watch, if even for a few moments. "Look!" the parent can point out, "that's the kind of plie you are learning"... or "See how she looks so much like a swan..." Video taping the productions will allow parent and child to enjoy the special techniques over and over.

There are commercial video tapes, too. One of the most useful and entertaining is "The Children of Theatre Street" (available through Kultur, 121 Highway 36, W. Long Branch, NJ 07764), a documentary about the training of children at the Kirov School in Leningrad, Russia. The lucky ones, of course, graduate into the world-famous Kirov Ballet, and for the beginning dancer it is important to see that what they are being asked to do in class is hardly different from what little Russian children are doing in *their* classes. The fact that the ultimate payoff may be as a company member in the Kirov Ballet won't be lost on many. A full catalog of dance videos is available from The Dance Book Club.

Various commercial video tapes and other ballet knickknacks can be found in general mail catalogs such as that from The Music Stand, 85 Mechanic St., Lebanon, New Hampshire. These catalogs list hundreds of items for every age group, and sometimes a simple tee shirt or lamp shade with a twirling ballerina superimposed will continue the spark set off inside the ballet studio.

Underlying all of this, of course, is the fact that ballet is but one form of dance and that all the dance forms have certain similarities. It is the expression of movement that is common, and for the beginning dancer it is important to remember that demonstrations of folk dancing, for instance, or square dancing, even clogging, are but variations on a general theme. Dance is a social event — people enjoy doing it and watching it together. It is not just arduous studio exercise without seeming purpose.

For the little one, then, ballet may not be a way of life — yet — but it lives outside the studio walls, and the parent who encourages this perception in the beginning dancer will find ample rewards as the dancer's skills burgeon inside the studio.

Part II:

The Recital Trap

Dancing a children's part with a professional company is an alternative to a recital performance.

The center spread of the local paper fairly leaps out. There is a large photo of a dance teacher, in black leotard with matching skirt, facing eight little tots, each costumed in tutu and ballet slippers. The teacher has her arms outstretched, her feet in first position. The faces of her diminutive dancers show rapt attention and determination.

Along the side of the floor — uncropped from the photo — are stray legs, knees and arms, undoubtedly fond parents, grandparents, siblings and friends who have come to witness a dance performance by a group of six-year-olds.

The caption under the photo reads: "Semi-annual recital of the local children's ballet class. Teacher and students ready to begin."

When it's over, among the comments will be the following:

"Aren't they cute!"

"They seem to love their teacher."

"So many nice things they are learning."

"Isn't it good they can perform so young!"

There are other predictable responses, too, because, in truth, the little tots *are* cute. Who could resist healthy, cheerful, bouncy, costumed little ones with the flush of excitement across

33

their faces? Who could resist a touch of pride in a six-year old striving to master one of the most beautiful, most delicate art forms? Who could resist approving the opportunity for a little one to perform, knowing that the art form is most viable when it can be offered to an audience?

This is the trap — the recital trap. Even though it seems as if dance training should lead to performance, no matter what the age, the facts are otherwise. The recital push, instead of helping the child's training, actually sets it back. Preparing for a recital is *not* the best way for a diminutive dancer to learn the art of ballet.

Listen to Rochelle McReynolds of the Boston Ballet who has choreographed for the stage, films and television. Recitals drive her "crazy" even if they do give the student a chance to perform. "When I have to do a recital," she says, "I'm thinking more about getting multiple material out there than doing quality material, and the student is getting only a little smattering of how best to interpret what is being done." If she had more time to work with individual students and to concentrate on the choreography and how to interpret it, the students "can grow with the piece to the end, and then I come away from that much more satisfied with their performance."

What she means, of course, is that the process of learning is infinitely more valuable than the end product — at least at an early age. But if performance is the major criteria, then something has to give, and unfortunately what falls away is control and understanding of the dance form. The young child simply learns less about the essential rudiments of ballet in favor of pleasing parents, grandparents and assorted others who stand to be thrilled by a six-year-old following dance movements that she — or he — have little understanding about.

It isn't only parents and grandparents that can land in the recital trap. Dance teachers are equally susceptible.

Some years ago I took over another dance teacher's school. This woman had put on an annual recital, and I figured I'd go along with it, at least for the first year. Mothers, grandmothers, aunts, sisters and neighbors spent hours sewing ribbon onto bits of chiffon, fathers lugged scenery and sound equipment around, a stage was hired, a backdrop rented. Parents took tickets at the door, grandmothers came with cameras and high anticipation at seeing their little ones perform. Everyone was excited, everyone was expectant.

All was wonderful... except the students couldn't dance! They knew few steps, little ballet terminology and had only a vague sense of the nature of classical ballet. They had spent five months learning the dance they would perform at their recital, and only minimal time with the general techniques of the art form.

It took three years, but the parents finally saw my point. Now, we spend only a few weeks on rehearsals, and we present a studio performance at the end of the year. Low-keyed, simple, yet expressive. We save the bulk of our class time during the year for learning — not rehearsing.

A number of dance studios or ballet schools still believe in the recital, and there's no denying it has some use. Since ballet is a performing art, the recital does provide that opportunity — though the age of the children involved make it of uncertain benefit. With all that family in the audience, the recital can be the least frightening performing alternative for a little dancer, but frequently the costs get out of hand. In some of the larger suburban ballet schools, each student can be cast in a minimum of two "numbers" and this means costumes (even ordered from a catalog it can easily reach $30-$50 for each one) and new shoes (which probably won't fit in three months). Now and then a school will insist that the children have their hair set and make-up applied by a professional beauty attendant!

Of course, there is the audience. *The parents.* Guess who buys tickets for family members — aunts and uncles, grandparents, siblings etc.? Don't forget the neighbors, the child's best friends, even a favorite regular school teacher... on and on.

But the recital must be a success, so any unsold tickets are bought by... guess who?

By now the parents are awash in all the recital details, and realization dawns that regular ballet class expenses are only *part* of what it takes to provide the proper ballet experience. And still the child may not be learning the right way.

Consider what Robert Barnett, Artistic Director of the Atlanta Ballet, says. "If I had my druthers, I'd never have recitals — they are strictly for the parents. It's much better to have lecture-demonstrations in the studio." He thinks recitals are a product of parent demand rather than the children's wish. "Parents insist on them," he says, "not the kids." In his school there are no recitals at all for the youngest children, aged five to seven. "It's an unnecessary expense with the costumes and the costume handling fees," he maintains, though he does provide for recitals when the students are between eight and twelve years of age. By then they have learned the rudiments of ballet and performing is now part of their training. At age thirteen the students "can join our second company — AB2 — if they have the talent."

Even as the child grows, however, the recital experience can hold them back. Studio dance training is only one opportunity for the young dancer, but there are others — including the regional ballet experience. (We'll explore this in greater depth in Part V, Ch. 4). Here the dancer is part of a semi-professional dance company which performs, but which also takes regular class. The emphasis is less on performing than on learning, and the results show. According to Ruth Ambrose, Dance Director at the Boston Conservatory, and someone who has been judging dance talent for a number of years, "Those that come out of the regional ballet experience already have some classical ballet background, while the ones who come from recital training have to go back and start from the

By eight years of age, performing is part of the training in some schools.

beginning. Dancers are really far ahead with a good regional ballet background than with a purely recital background."

But recitals continue to abound. "Look at me, Mom!" is both a classic motivation and a classic misapplication. Parents see them as a report card on how their children are doing and as a reward for encouraging artistic expression; children see recitals as the ultimate payback for coping with the regular demands of ballet class. In both cases the real point is overlooked: ballet requires intensive training and application, it is not made less arduous nor more expressive by a recital. In fact, recitals can give a false sense of achievement with "Look at me, Mom!" the goal instead of a simple statement that some progress has been made.

If a student believes that going on stage is a reward for attending class, a major element of professionalism will have been lost. It will be exceedingly difficult for the student to understand that a professional artist has a sacred respect for the physical stage and that stage appearances are the result of talent and extremely hard work — not the simple reward of good attendance and good attention. A good ballet school trains its students to view the stage — whether it is the Lincoln Center, a local high school or a town meeting hall — as the ultimate goal of training, and the dancers who perform there are those who have worked the hardest and who have developed their talent to a point where performing is an appropriate reward.

But if there *must* be a recital, then it is wise to heed the words of Doris Herring, former director of the National Association of Regional Ballets, and someone who has worked with young dancers and their studios for years. "One piece of advice I have for parents," she says, "is that it is important to watch classes, to see how the children are responding, that they aren't being pulled beyond their level, that they are comfortable in the class, and that they are all participating. *Make sure that not too much of the classroom time is taken up with preparing for recitals... that they are not denied their regular training while they are getting ready for a recital.*"

Part III:

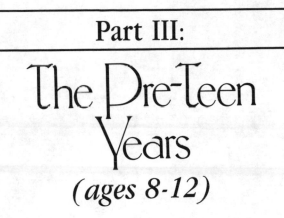

The Pre-Teen Years
(ages 8-12)

...from the first day of dance training, ballet class follows a definite format...

———————Chapter 1:———————
Learning the Childrens'
Ballet Syllabus

Every school of ballet, every teacher of ballet has a plan of instruction (called a syllabus), and it is the essential ingredient in all ballet instruction. This plan of instruction operates from the first day a wary four-year-old enters the studio and carries forward, week after week, month after month, year after year, until an accomplished seventeen- or eighteen-year-old proudly exhibits his or her first company contract. The syllabus informs teacher and student, parent and director what has been learned, what will be learned, when and how. It is a road map of lesson plans that will take raw, undeveloped talent and turn it into graceful, expressive ballet years into the future.

Every ballet parent, every ballet child should be familiar with the ballet syllabus their teacher follows. There should be no surprises, no uncertainties.

Begin with this... *discipline*. Ballet class means discipline. It means attending class day after day through each level of instruction. It means giving up certain pleasures such as a best friend's birthday party, or a quick visit to grandmother; it means listening and following the teacher; it means being serious about the art.

Listen to Agnes de Mille, one of our greatest choreographers. She writes: "Never miss the daily practice, hell or high water, sickness or health. Never miss the barre practice. Miss meals, sleep, rehearsal even, but not the practice, not for one day, ever, under any circumstances . . ."

Tough stuff to lay on an eight-year-old and perhaps a bit too demanding for that young age. But the principle is clear . . . discipline is what should drive the young dancer, and it's never too early to learn that! For the parent the important thing is to realize that as the child grows the discipline will become more encompassing, more insistent. The young dancer's ballet school syllabus will be founded upon it.

From the first day of dance training (following the creative dance and pre-ballet experiences), ballet class follows a definite format, and this will not vary no matter the teacher, the school, or the level of training. Class always begins with exercises at the barre, then continues with stretching and centre work. Then follows an adagio, pirouettes, petit allegros, grand allegros and fast turning or jumps. The normal class runs from one to one and one-half hours and concludes with a bow or curtsy (called a reverance).

Eight-year-olds certainly can't perform all these movements, and the appropriate ballet syllabus takes that into account. But the classes are structured so that each movement can be the success point the children strive for.

There are a number of basic ballet syllabuses, some more prominent in Europe, some more closely followed in the United States. Most are excellent because they have stood the test of time, developing ballet dancers through the decades and providing rigid standards through which to judge the art and its practitioners. Among the more prevalent syllabuses in the United States are the Royal Academy of Dancing (British), Cecchetti (Italian) and Vaganova (Russian), all of which teach not only ballet steps but also the rules of ballet, such as the correct positions of the head, arms, legs and feet and the directions of the body in relation to the studio or stage. It's important to note this difference because ballet is much more than a basic routine of dance steps, it is a full artistic experience.

Bruce Marks, artistic director of the Boston Ballet, is adamant on this point, and he feels that a concentration on the mechanics of ballet at the expense of a broader purpose is ultimately harmful. "Often a dancer can do class, but it doesn't mean that dancer can dance; it means the dancer can do ballet class," he says, "and I find more and more that these classes do not relate to what we do on stage." For Marks the important thing is to teach students how to perform, not how to take a ballet class.

Yet even if one of these syllabuses is closely followed a creative teacher will adapt those portions she or he thinks are most useful and discard those that might not be appropriate. For example, Noble Barker, director of the New Haven (Connecticut) School of Ballet, says that the Vaganova syllabus "relates the work to what is done on stage" and that is fine for some dancers. But not for all. "The students who are really good get great, the students in the middle get hurt. There are a lot of kids out there that have enough ability but they get so discouraged by the forced turnout and all the relevé. So," he admits, "I just use the things I think are important."

There is a certain logic to the order that ballet movement is taught, and each syllabus stresses that progression. Some of the more common movements and the years in which they should be tried include:

First year — Simplified combinations of the basic exercises, such as demi plié in first, second, third positions.

Barre work, such as degagé ronde de jombe, passé, preparation for "grand battement" — or proper body placement is important here because bad habits picked up now could be impossible to correct later on.

Simple stretching exercises off the barre — should be practiced at home so muscles can maintain suppleness.

Once stretching exercises finish then comes "port de bras" taught with use of head, eyes and upper body for all five positions.

Second year — Full plié

Second, third year — 180 degree turnout of legs and feet, fifth position.

More complicated jumps, piroutes, head movement with adagio work.

Other movements such as multiple pirouttes, waltzes, moving steps, gallops and big jumps follow along during these initial years, but each has its place in the syllabus and will not be explored until the young dancer is prepared. It's interesting to note, though, that the ballet tradition has established these movements in a proper sense of order. Any urge to mix them up will show why . . .

Just ask Marcia Dale Weary, artistic director of the Central Pennsylvania Youth Ballet. "I usually teach pirouttes from second position," (feet approximately 18" apart sideways) she says, "and one time someone said 'why don't you try that from fourth or fifth position?' (one foot in front of the other) It seemed like a good idea so I tried it, but it just didn't work. Second position is best for pirouttes because the students can feel themselves springing up and bringing their leg in better."

No parent, absent a prior dance career, could be expected to know and understand the many details in a ballet syllabus. Nor is it necessary for that to take place. A good teacher should be able to point to the syllabus she or he is following and to interpret it properly so young dancers will have a firm, valuable grounding in the art. Parents should be able to rely on a good teacher for this.

There are, however, certain things a parent can do that will profit a budding ballet career. The esoteric aspects of a syllabus notwithstanding, parents should be on the lookout to make sure that the *craft* of ballet is being taught:

— are the legs and feet being forced to turn out?

— are the knees in line with the toes?

— are the children being made to listen carefully to the music? They should develop their sense of musicality now because it is important in later years.

These pre-teen years are probably the most important of a dancer's training. It is between the ages of eight through twelve that the basics of ballet are learned, and these will form the foundation for an ultimate professional career. Attention, discipline, careful execution and a good ballet teacher are what it will take. Parents have to be involved because young dancers need extraordinary guidance as they immerse themselves in this encompassing art form.

And a parent who understands the value of a ballet syllabus will be a participant in their young dancer's blossoming talent.

It takes many months of pointe work before a student executes a relevé on one foot.

Chapter 2

Going "on pointe" —
How and Why

If a lovely sound is one mark of a cherished songbird, then unadorned grace is one mark — for some, *the* mark — of an accomplished ballet dancer. Grace above all because it presents beauty and style and elegance with seeming effortlessness, spurring the art form to ever higher accomplishment. Grace is sought in movement, in stage presence, in costuming ... in total performance. It is a ballet benchmark.

What better way, then, to approach graceful performance by molding the graceful ballet body into an instrument that moves gracefully and performs the most graceful steps?

And what is more lovely than a graceful body fully extended and balanced confidently on a tiny point of toe space? It is symmetry with the charm of color and shape, perfect proportions of beauty and skill.

The dancer "on pointe".

Not easy to learn, even more difficult to master. But essential for the young ballet dancer. There is no classical ballet work that does not require some dancing on pointe. It is as much a part of the ballet dancer's training and repertoire as an arabesque body position or a port de bras arm position.

First things first. Only girls dance "on pointe". Boys never do. One reason is that female musculature develops differently; male dancers are built in such a way that pointe work is almost impossible. Another reason is based on that unceasing search for grace and the fact that femininity flowers as the female form minces and twirls and settles. Pointe training is directed at girls, and it is as much a beginning dancer's rite of passage to advance status as any other thing in her ballet training.

Once the young dancer faces pointe work, the serious business of ballet has really begun.

Age has relatively little to do with readiness for it. Leg and body development are the keys, and the teacher must be the one who makes the decision. A good teacher will look for:

— strong feet

— a graceful line from ankle to toe

— the toe pointed, not curled, when stretched

— the use of muscles on top of the foot as well as those under the arches

— straight and strong legs, knees and thighs in proper alignment

— the satorious muscle (in the thigh) visible and well developed when the young dancer is in releve, or sitting on the floor, legs apart and stretching

— a straight spine

— strong abdominal muscles

Generally, the first exposure to pointe work will not come until the latter part of the second or third training year when the students have been developing along a constant, well-structured path. Careful preparation is so important!

The initial exercises will not last more than five to ten minutes, and they are usually given at the end of class because they represent a major departure from anything the young dancers have learned before. And they are hard to do . . . and sometimes they hurt!

One big problem: because the early pointe work is introduced near the end of the year, many young dancers take it upon themselves to practice, practice, practice during the summer. *This is not a good idea* unless there is expert supervision handy.

The reason? Practice without direction can be injurious, even dangerous. Without sufficient knowledge the young dancer is unable to make the proper body and placement corrections, and should she escape injury, she runs the real risk of learning improper movements that must then be unlearned when she resumes classes in the fall . . . assuming she hasn't already developed muscle habits that might be impossible to redirect.

The key to pointe work, of course, is proper pointe shoes (see the next chapter for a thorough discussion). The teacher should be the main guide here, and once the shoes have been bought, the teacher should check the fit carefully. A snug fit is essential, anything less can bring toe blisters and possible ruin to ankles, legs and feet by destroying tendons and ligaments.

It should be obvious, then, that pointe shoes must *not* be bought with an eye towards the child's future growth. Pointe shoes must be for *now,* not a year or two from now. If they are to be used, they must fit the moment.

The pointe shoe, when properly worn, is secured by ribbons that circle the ankle and lower leg. These ribbons are not part of the shoe when it is bought, and many teachers ask that parents avoid sewing on the ribbons for their child. "Learning to sew the ribbon on the shoe is an integral part of the training," says one well-known teacher. "Every dancer — the famous as well as the beginner — has her own special way to prepare her shoe; it becomes a personal ritual."

The initial pointe class, therefore, resembles less an hour of dance instruction and more a period of manual arts. "Bring a needle, heavy duty cotton thread, scissors, ribbons and elastic," the teacher will say. "We're going to learn to prepare our pointe shoes."

Slowly the work proceeds, and finally the shoes are adorned and fitted. "Slip them on," the teacher says. "Be sure they feel snug." There is joy on every face.

When my daughter was ten years old, she and
the rest of her ballet class were allowed to buy their
first pointe shoes. A local shoe store brought dozens

of pairs to the studio, and as each child was fitted, she dashed home joyfully clutching the precious pink satin shoes.

Finally, only my daughter, the salesman and I were left in the studio. None of the new shoes fitted my daughter's narrow foot. Tears welled in her eyes, and the salesman shook his head sadly. Then I remembered . . . there were some pointe shoes in the costume shop. A friend had given them to me when his store went out of business.

We found them, stained from age but unused. My daughter slipped them on, and the fit was perfect. A beautiful smile replaced the tears. She took my hand, rose on pointe — unsteadily to be sure — and, to my horror, ran out of the studio, across the lawn and into the house.

To show Dad. "I'm on pointe," she told him, her little legs wobbly and insecure.

But the old, stained pointe shoes held her aloft for a few beautiful seconds.

For the first few months the major pointe exercises will be at the barre, holding on with both hands and practicing relevés (slow rises through the ball of the foot onto the tip of the toe) in four of the five basic positions (1st, 2nd, 4th and 5th). Only after the young dancer is able to roll slowly on and off pointe with her whole foot, similar to the way she uses her feet in battement tendu, can the next progression be tried . . . a relevé on one foot . . . and then additional progressions will be added, as each prior one is mastered . . . echappes, temps lies, piques and finally the pas de bourree . . . Any doubt that pointe work can be excruciatingly difficult needs only to hear Lupe Serrano, one of the foremost ballerinas in the United States. She calls the pas de bourree "the hardest step ever invented," saying she would rather "do 32 fouettes or a series of entrechat-six than cross the stage in pas de bourree."

But all of that is far in the future for the young dancer. For the first year it is unlikely any pointe work will take place without the barre. If the teacher does take her students off the barre, it will be for simple bourrees and temps lie using both feet. No one-footed steps yet.

Then, in the second year, more complicated steps at the

barre will be practiced, and preparations for pirouettes and balances can be started . . .

But pointe work can't be rushed. It is too difficult and too demanding to expect any form of immediate gratification. True ballet grace is only achieved through constant work and training, and as with most beautiful art forms, what we as spectators see is but the culmination of arduous effort, extensive learning and talent honed through dedication and patience.

"She is so graceful," we might say, as the lovely ballerina glides on pointe across the stage.

But it isn't easy, and it isn't simple.

Body placement is the most important part of a dancer's training.

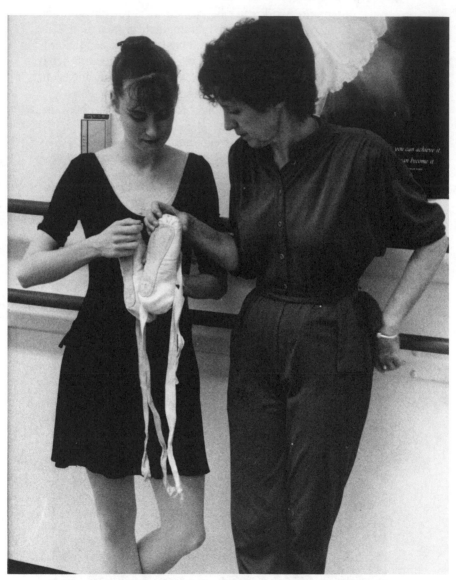

Pointe shoes must be constantly checked.

Chapter 3:

All About Pointe Shoes

A mother's first reaction: "My God! You'll ruin your feet."

"Oh, Mother! ..." The young dancer shakes her head. "All ballet dancers wear pointe shoes."

The mother grimaces. "They look so awkward, such a strange toe, such little support along the sides. I don't see how they hold you up ..."

"Oh, Mother! ..."

The truth is the pointe shoe does its job well and efficiently, even if it looks like something more appropriate for punishment. Hard, square toe ... flimsy sides ... ribbon and elastic that drawn tight can cut off circulation ... an unforgiving narrow sole. A former student used to call them "pretty pink satin torture chambers."

Definitely not for aerobics.

Dancing "on pointe" has a long history, and the first shoes were probably designed so the dancer could surpass the tiptoe grace that even modest training might achieve. If the dancer could truly rise to the pinnacle of her foot arch, the body could become an unbroken line, an element of perfection, throughout.

Enter the pointe shoe. It goes back at least 200 years,

to the time of Marie Taglioni whose early 19th-century performances were the toast of Europe. Ballet lore has it that she was
the first to rise on pointe, (some historians make a case that
others preceded her) though there is doubt that she actually
danced in this position. More likely, she posed on pointe, returning
to the usual ballet shoe when movement was required. In fact,
her original pointe shoes have been preserved, and it's obvious
they were not designed for any demanding choreography. They
were simply not sturdy enough.

But even if Taglioni was the first to rise on pointe, the
practice was not uniformly adopted. It took years before the corps
de ballet would follow along, and it took still more years before
the corps would dance — rather than pose — on pointe.

Now, of course, dancing on pointe is an integral part of
any dancer's training, and through the generations the pointe shoe
has been transformed into a marvelously precise instrument. The
right shoe can work wonders for the right dancer. It is as much
a part of the dancer's art as an exquisite arabesque or a soaring
grand jeté.

But what of the pointe shoe? What should we know? To
start with, the following terms should be understood:

Box — The stiffened part of the shoe that encases the
toes.

Pointe — The art of rising to the tip of the toe.

Vamp — The part of the box, from the top of the toes
to the underside where pleating meets sole.

Shank — The inner sole.

Pleating — The satin drawn over the front of the toe
and folded under the toe where it is joined to the sole.

Darning — Embroidering the tip of the toe and the
pleats with silk thread.

Ribbons — One-half-inch-wide satin pieces attached to
the shoe with a "grosgrain" or rougher texture on the
reverse side.

The Pointe Shoe

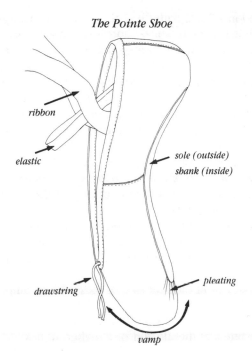

These are the pointe shoe basics, and as we discuss some of the variations in different designs and materials, we will see that most variations occur here. One box — or one shank — or one pleating — will differ from another because the manufacturer will want to emphasize one purpose more than another, but it should be clear that all the manufacturers seek the same goal — a shoe that will make dancing on pointe a joyous, graceful and comfortable exercise.

Compare the shoe that Marie Taglioni wore so many years ago. It had no hardened box (thus making it difficult to rise on pointe). It had flexible leather soles (thus making it difficult to hold a pointe), silk satin tops and darning along the sides and under the pointe (thus increasing the sturdiness of the over-all shoe, but not the pointe area). It's obvious she could not have stayed on pointe long.

A certain myth surrounds pointe shoes — that they have wood or steel in the toes. Nothing could be less true. Much of the construction on pointe shoes is done by hand, master cobblers following generations-old techniques. The top of the shoe is made of layers of canvas and satin (great ballerinas such as Margot Fonteyn of London's Royal Ballet had the top layer made from pure silk because it was more sturdy and less slippery than synthetic satin). The upper part of the shoe — made of satin — wraps around and under the foot and is attached to a stiff, narrow sole, and the cobbler uses a special tool to pleat the satin before sewing it to the sole because there cannot be any bumpy or ragged edges in the satin which could throw the dancers' balance off.

On top, the many layers of canvas are glued together to create the box, and a drawstring runs around the outer edge of the shoe so that the dancer can adjust it to fit her foot snugly and comfortably. It is the box that the dancer rises onto when going on pointe, and if there is any uncertainty in the fit, the pointe position will disintegrate.

And there is no wood or metal anywhere!

Professional dancers, of course, take the basic pointe shoe and customize it to suit their own designs. They might:

— cut down on the box size or extend the vamp.

— cut down the shoe sides because it can give a prettier line and the illusion of a higher arch.

— have the heels cut up higher so the shoe won't slip off.

— have a lighter sole or a shorter shank.

Customizing one's shoes means that every pair has to be specially ordered from the manufacturer. For the young student dancer this may mean added expense and the possibility that significant time delays might be experienced, thus affecting class time and proper training. Even for professionals this can mean problems:

> *When I worked with the Atlanta Ballet, one dancer insisted on special-order Gamba shoes from England. I had ordered them for her in August and by the first performances of Nutcracker — in November — they still hadn't arrived. Numerous phone calls to the Gamba store in London had proved unavailing.*
>
> *Finally, I tried to find her a close substitute*

even as we began touring. In airport after airport I called local and national shoe suppliers, but there was nothing suitable. First, she would dance in one brand, then another, never comfortable, never settled. And, of course, her dancing suffered because her feet hurt.

Then, with only six performances left, the Gamba shoes arrived. Joyfully, she put them on and started to dance... only to wither in pain because her feet no longer found them compatible. The other shoe varieties had changed her technique.

What shoe to buy, then? The young dancer's teacher is the first place to check. The teacher should know.

Most importantly, there is a correct shoe for every dancer... *but it may differ from dancer to dancer!* Not everyone should wear the same kind of shoe.

Why? Because the shoe type depends on the structure of the dancer's foot, and some types of shoes are more appropriate for one configuration, other types for another. There are, however, certain pointe shoe brands that offer special characteristics:

Capezio — the most readily available shoes in the United States, providing eight different strengths and pointe shoe shapes.

Frederick Freed — the most popular European shoe, made of a peach-colored satin, much lighter weight and more flexible than Capezio styles; should not be used until the dancer has developed a strong foot.

Bloch — a relatively new and lightweight shoe, it is recommended for the more advanced dancer.

Wasner and Schakner — German shoes with the box made of fiberglass instead of glued canvas; some controversy about these shoes, but they do have a longer life because the box does not wear out.

Eva Martin — square-toed and fine for balancing and turning; can be bought from stock with a choice of hard or soft shanks; especially useful because the more durable, hard shanks can be used in class, soft shanks in performance.

Chacotte — a Japanese shoe not readily available throughout the United States; it is lightweight and well constructed.

The shoes are chosen and bought. Now comes customizing . . .

A mother's reaction: "You are destroying that beautiful shoe!"

"Oh, Mother! I'm breaking them in."

The back center seam is pushed down inside the sole, bending it beyond seeming capability.

"It's ripping!"

"Mother!"

Needle and thread in her hand, the young dancer begins to sew a piece of ribbon onto the shoe fold.

"That's not ordinary thread."

"It's heavy-duty cotton," the young dancer says, not looking up. "Some people use dental floss instead."

"Ugh!"

"The ribbon's important. It wraps above our ankles and gives support when we're on pointe."

"Now what are you doing?"

Pieces of elastic — about three-quarters of an inch wide — are attached to the back of the shoe. The young dancer slips her foot under the elastic so it is stretched over her instep.

"Won't that stop your blood circulation?"

"Oh, Mother! It's so my shoe won't slip off." The young dancer shakes her head. "Don't you understand *anything?*"

"I don't want you to be hurt, dear, that's all." The mother picks up the other shoe and examines the toe point. There is heavy darning stitch about an inch square. "What's this for?"

"My pointe work. It's like a cushion, and it prevents slipping when I'm working on a wooden floor . . ."

If the mother isn't mystified by this time, she soon will be when the young dancer breaks the shoes in. It isn't enough to customize them, they must now be molded to the feet.

"What are you doing?" The mother is appalled as the young dancer has stuck her shoes in the door jamb and is slamming the door on them. "I paid $37.50 for those."

"I'm trying to soften the box." Slam! . . . slam! . . . slam! . . .

Another mother might have an equal reaction as her young dancer fills her new pointe shoes with alcohol, swishes the liquid around, then pours it out, slips the shoes on and walks around until they dry.

"It smells awful in here! Did you spill something?"

"My shoes need breaking in . . ."

Or a father may be seeking his upholstery hammer, only to find his young dancer using it to whack against the pleating of her new pointe shoes.

"You're destroying a brand new shoe. Are you insane?"

"I'm trying to make them quieter. They scratch and rustle when they're new."

"I never heard of such a thing."

Thwack! . . . thwack! . . . thwack! . . .

Breaking them in. The techniques are as varied as the imaginations of the young dancers. The purpose? Singular: so the pointe shoe is integral to the dancer's foot.

Of course, pointe shoes don't last long. A prima ballerina can use as many as three pairs in a single four-act performance such as Swan Lake or Sleeping Beauty. A corps de ballet member will average one to two pairs per week during heavy rehearsal and performance periods. An advanced dancer will use a pair every ten days to two weeks, and a young beginning student can usually make a pair last for one semester.

There is a ritual in getting the pointe shoe ready to be worn and in putting it on . . .

First comes surgical tape. Dancers wrap each toe separately to avoid rubbing and blisters. Then they wrap lambs wool or paper towels around their toes and feet to lessen rubbing. But they *never, ever* wad lambs wool or toweling inside the shoe first. It will cause lumps and . . . blisters.

Then . . . a trip to the rosin box where the stockinged heel is emersed thoroughly, followed by a light dousing of water to insure the foot will not slip out of the pointe shoe. (Some more creative young dancers have used a spot of commercial glue on the heel to do the same job.)

Slip the shoe on, cross the ribbons over and around the ankle and tie a neat knot behind the ankle bone. Be careful, though . . . *never, ever* put the knot on the achilles tendon. It should be tucked into the ribbon to avoid rubbing and chaffing and present a clean, sleek line.

And when the young dancer is performing, she, herself, will sew the ribbon knot to the ribbon so it will not loosen.

A mother's further reaction: "So many little things to remember. I never realized."

"My foot's no different than the rest of my body," the young dancer answers. "The more beautiful my foot, the more beautiful my body . . . the more beautiful my body, the more beautiful my dancing."

"I still think the shoes look strange."

"Oh, Mother! . . ."

Pointe shoes must be customized to fit the structure of the dancer's foot.

——————Chapter 4:——————
The Ballet Body

A body is a body is a body . . . To most of us, special body types are meaningful only in the context of what is attractive or unattractive. "Look at that body!" a 19-year-old male might remark about a female counterpart, and we wouldn't have much trouble understanding to what he is referring. "I love his body," a co-ed on the beach might say about a husky lifeguard, and there would be nods all around. Of course we understand.

"Beautiful" is a body word. It raises an image in our minds, something we can picture. And the view is probably a bit different for each of us. The beautiful body. Female movie stars used to vie for such a designation. "The body beautiful" one was called, or, more simply, "The Body"! We knew then what it meant, we know now what it means.

At least as it applies in a general way. Once we narrow our focus, though, "beautiful" takes on conditions and restrictions. A weight lifter has a beautiful body, for example, when the strength muscles bulge and pop, but for any other purpose such a body might lose its appeal. A swimmer with weight lifter's muscles would hardly have a beautiful swimmer's body because the supple leanness that all swimmers cultivate would no longer be evident.

So it is with the ballet body. Beauty is not a term to be applied loosely, and the beautiful ballet body is not the same thing as the beautiful body. "A beautiful body by society's standards," says Robert Lindgren, director of the School of American Ballet, "is not a beautiful body by ballet standards." What he means is that the ballet body must conform to certain special, narrow conditions that may or may not be appealing to the generalized public view. What he also means is that someone with "The Body Beautiful" would not qualify for ballet body kudos. Ballet requires something different.

How different? Quite a bit it seems, and the answer is elusive enough without adding the individual tastes and preferences of particular artistic directors who recognize the basic ballet body but then seek to remold it to suit their own artistic eye. Some, for example, place limits on height; others place limits on body structure (Thin! Thin! Thin!); still others seek a slightly more voluptuous form. It isn't that these requirements are so varied; it is, rather, the individual expression of the artistic director that creates the art form.

We can see it wherever ballet is performed these days. Over the past three or four decades a truly American ballet body has emerged, and the primary source for its development was George Balanchine, the late artistic director of the New York City Ballet. Balanchine had a love for the long, leggy dancer who was thin, thin, thin! And because of his influence, this body type became the standard by which the ballet body would be judged, not only with the New York City Ballet, but elsewhere as well.

Other directors might add their own special limitations such as with height or form, but the leggy dancer, that never varied.

The American ballet body.

Do we seek perfection? Never attainable, of course, but the "proper" ballet body, based on the Balanchine influence and allowing for individual artistic director variations would — or should — resemble the following:

— height: between 5'2" and 5'8"

— long, slender legs, straight and tapering

— small, flat buttocks and hips

— narrow waist

— flat abdomen and diaphram

— small bust

— long neck and small head, perfectly set on shoulders

— graceful, smooth-muscled arms

— soft, fluid hands and fingers

Suppose it's the male body we're dealing with? Even here there are some definite standards:

— height: between 5'8" and 6'2"

— long, tapering legs, proportionate feet and hands

— slender hips and waist, strong, broad chest

— strong arms and back (to execute the dynamic lifts)

— lythe and supple

The American ballet body. But don't think this is carved in stone. Times change, body styles change. What is proper form in one era may be unacceptable in another. Listen to Doris Herring, former director of the National Association of Regional Ballets, a teacher and choreographer: "Probably the Balanchine influence will diminish as time goes on," she says. "Weight and body are a matter of style or fashion. I look at pictures of dancers in the 1930's, and they look so fat to me, but that was the style then."

If she's right, then the ballet body of today should not be taken as an absolute for the decades ahead. And the dancer who might not fit snugly within the picture should not feel discouraged. The American dancer is taller and more elongated than European dancers, and the requirements for the ballet body in Europe make allowance for this. Many a shorter American dancer, trained only in the United States, has gone to Europe and found a ready place in a company even while no place would exist in the United States. A male dancer who is six-foot-four inches, a female dancer at five foot should not assume that their ballet bodies are inappropriate in the ballet world; they need search long enough to find a proper fit.

Sometimes, though, it can seem terribly frustrating:

From the time I decided to become a dancer, at age eight, I had my heart set on joining the Royal Ballet in London. Nothing else would satisfy me, and I trained and trained with this in mind. One day when I was twelve, I went into the studio to find that our teacher was measuring all of us. I had grown tremendously in the past year, and it unsettled me. Was I becoming too tall?

There are definite standards to the male dancer's body.

My worst fears were realized. I was now five-foot-five inches, and my wished-for career with the Royal Ballet was shattered. I would not even be able to audition for them. The tears flowed for weeks.

Why? Because Margot Fonteyn, prima ballerina of the Royal Ballet, was five-foot-four inches, and it was common knowledge that no one was hired for the company if they were taller than she. Company policy, no exceptions. The prima ballerina could tower over the other dancers, but never, never could a company dancer tower over the prima!

The American ballet body.

The search for the proper ballet body begins in the early years, of course, because that is when the good eating and exercise habits will become ingrained, and the child's body will react positively to this discipline. But even at ages seven or eight, one can pick out the better ballet body. "I look for the good feet," says Marcia Dale Weary of the Central Pennsylvania Youth Ballet, adding that it's not useful to examine the entire leg because its form will change as the child grows older. "Maybe a little, slight hyperextension of the leg," could be examined, but it's limited. She looks for the way the young child moves, the graceful neck, the turnout... those elements of the ballet body that will remain fairly constant as the child grows.

Good teachers know how precarious it can be to make firm decisions about a child's ballet body. Not only do physical proportions change as the child grows, but even in the clearest negative instances, there can be surprises. "Sometimes," relates Lydia Joel, former head of dance with the New York City High School of the Performing Arts, "you get a little kid who looks like a dried mushroom, but then she begins to dance, and your heart goes out to her..."

There are few absolutes with the ballet body because tastes and styles are constantly evolving. The "perfection" of a generation ago disintegrates in the maze of current appeal, and it is readily certain that today's "perfection" will be remolded a generation from now. Yet the ballet body remains an instrument, first and foremost, an expression of the art form. What is proper, or improper, at any given moment rests in the eyes of the dance creator, and in order to prepare ourselves we must understand what has gone on before and what is acceptable today.

The Balanchine ballet body... long, lean, leggy....today it is the standard.

But tomorrow? We must wait and see.

The female and male body structure must complement each other in a pas de deux.

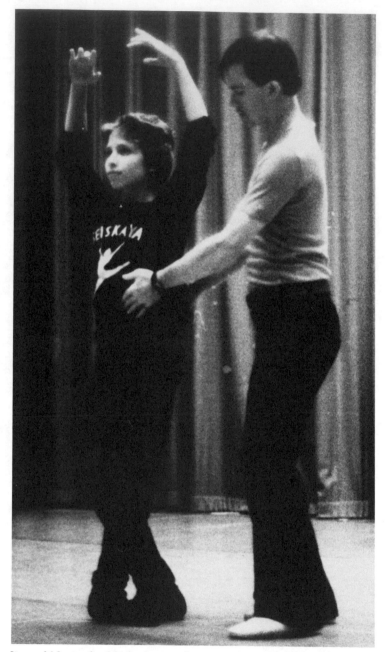

It would be preferable for boys to have a male teacher from age twelve.

----------Chapter 5:----------
Special Training
for Boys

Alexander Bennett, director of the Scottish-American Ballet, tells the story of his decision to learn ballet when he was seventeen years old. He was living in Leith, a small town in Scotland. "One afternoon in 1946, I went to the King's Theatre in Edinburgh to see Sadlers Wells Ballet, and I fell in love with the prima ballerina, Margot Fonteyn." He felt a sense of joy and completeness he had never experienced before.

"I realized that this was what I had wanted to do all my life."

Then came reality. Dance ballet? "Where in Leith could I possibly find help? Male ballet dancers were rare — to say the least — in my section of Scotland."

Rare, but necessary, of course. For Alexander Bennett, and for countless other male dancers before him, the ballet world had an outsized need. Males had to perform certain movements that required substantial strength; males had to partner females in such a way that the grace and beauty of classical ballet could be demonstrated clearly, cleanly and harmoniously.

Unfortunately, a half-century ago, boys did not embrace classical ballet in the numbers or with the rush of enthusiasm that young girls did. But that has changed now, and as their numbers have increased boys ballet training has become more prevalent and more important.

Stanley Williams of the School of American Ballet, perhaps the foremost ballet teacher for boys in this country, acknowledges the more difficult, earlier days and describes why boys need special training. "It used to be harder for the boys to dedicate themselves to ballet," he says, "and today that has all changed. It's acceptable for boys to be in ballet now. But they need to achieve enormous physical strength. Their success comes from making feats of incredible strength look like nothing."

Lifts, for example; the fish movement, the press lift.

Not arabesques, not bourrees or pointe work.

A major way boys' and girls' training differs is that with girls there is essential femaleness in the body movement, while with boys the emphasis is on strength, simple strength. Grace versus brawn, beauty versus power.

No surprise, then, that from an early age boys and girls at the larger professional schools are separated in classroom work. At the School of American Ballet, for example, boys go to their own classes from age twelve, and there they stay right through their training. Smaller schools, of course, and particularly those in more rural areas, find it difficult to set up special boys classes because of a narrower student pool and lack of experienced teachers and studio space. But that should not prevent boys from receiving training. It's perfectly appropriate for young boys to attend regular ballet classes with girls, even up to their mid-teens, so long as the boys' special training and moves are followed.

But note this:

— the teacher must continually stress the need for strength.

— the boy's "port de bras" (arm movements) should be developed to show strength and masculinity.

— it would be preferable to have a male teacher from age twelve on.

The major strength points for boys are in the torso, arms and legs. These are the areas that receive greatest pressure and greatest use, and they must be fully developed in order to provide clean partnering to the girls, to provide bravura jumps and leaps and to avoid injuries. How best to develop that strength? Nautilus and Pilates training are probably the most effective methods to strengthen the body through special exercise and/or machinery. The key is not to develop short, bulky muscles which can interrupt the clean lines on the dancer's body, thus affecting grace and beauty. Eddy Toussaint, director of the Ballet de Montreal, has his male dancers do push-ups regularly in order to build stamina and strength, yet avoid a stick-out musculature. "Push-ups," he feels, "are the natural way for the muscles to develop," and he makes sure his male dancers stay away from any weight lifting exercises. "Overdeveloped" is what he calls those who seek strength from weight lifting.

"Nautilus is good, push-ups are safe," he emphasizes. Strength and stamina and clean muscle line are the result.

Pointe training is another area where boys and girls separate. For the girls, of course, going "on pointe" is the culmination of years of training; for the boys there is no similar rite of passage. Boys do not dance on pointe. Never, ever. But they can —and sometimes do — take pointe classes. They wear their regular dance shoes and they follow the girl's exercises by going on "demi-pointe," that is by raising themselves on one-half toe. Why? Because it will help develop feet and ankles. It will give them added strength.

But under no circumstances should boys wear pointe shoes. Their feet are not trained for them. Their bodies are built differently. They don't have the same type of muscles, and injuries and accidents could develop.

The purpose of special classes and training for boys is to concentrate on those things boys must do — such as lift turns and bravura jumps — that will enhance the beauty and grace of the ballet art form. Though the boys' emphasis on strength and stamina is far different than the girl's emphasis on delicate and breathtaking form, ultimately each concentration must blend with the other if true art is to result. Boys and girls are *partners*. After all, ballet is a melding of that partnership. Stanley Williams knows this, and that is why he can say, "I give company classes where there are both sexes, and I have to teach these classes in such a way that both sexes get something they need."

Together and separate, but the same goal for both.

Part IV:

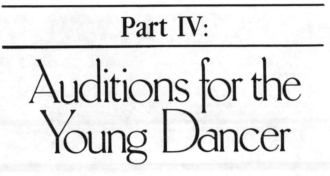

Auditions for the
Young Dancer

Anticipating the results at the audition for party children in the first act of the "Nutcracker".

It's a fact of life in the ballet world... auditions are the way we choose dancers. It's a process that starts at a tender age and will be repeated periodically until the student decides some other career beckons.

Even if the student becomes a professional, and even if the professional retires to teach ballet, the world of the audition is ever-present. It is a foundation of the ballet experience.

And it is never too early to learn about, and be exposed to, auditions. "There's a tremendous amount of value in the opportunity for children to audition with a major company," says Madeline Cantrella Culpo, artistic director of the Berkshire Ballet Theatre in Pittsfield, Massachusetts. "To work with professional dancers, to have a chance to get on stage and to experience the thrill of a live ballet performance, is so important."

It's not an easy process, of course, no matter what the age. For young children it might be the first serious competition they will have faced, yet if they intend to pursue dance into their teens — or, especially, if they decide to make ballet a career — they are going to come against auditioning again and again, and it is best if they get an early exposure to it.

Usually, the first opportunity for a young dancer to audition is for the annual Christmas production of "Nutcracker." Most versions of this popular favorite use children as soldiers, candy canes, party children, angels and reindeer. The story deals with a toy nutcracker given to a young girl, Clara, and subsequently broken by her brother. In a dream, Clara's concern for the broken toy is rewarded by her magical "uncle" who takes the child through a Snow Forest to the Kingdom of Sweets. Here the "candies" from many countries dance for Clara, and the dream is brought to a climax by the dance of the Sugar Plum Fairy and her Cavalier.

Many companies use the same children for years, first as reindeer, then as angels, party children and so forth. As the children grow, they are promoted to another role in each succeeding annual production. The large, professional ballet companies give thirty or more performances in the weeks preceding Christmas, while the smaller companies may only perform a few times, even though the casts can be up to one hundred and more. For the larger companies such as the Boston Ballet, Pacific Northwest Ballet and New York City Ballet, pickings are easier because they can choose children from their own ballet schools.

Even so, auditions for the roles in "Nutcracker" are held each year, regardless of whether the company is large or small.

And the young dancers start very young indeed! "How young we audition children for "Nutcracker" is different from how young they should be," admits Madeline Cantrella Culpo, who is, nevertheless, resigned to the reality of things. "They seem to sneak in at five years old, though we think six to eight years old is the bottom limit. Then, too, some six-year-olds are not ready for auditioning or performing, so it's hard to make an unqualified rule."

Alexander Bennett, director of the Scottish-American Ballet in Normal, Illinois, would agree. For him a five-year-old angel "doesn't take direction from Heaven very well," and he doesn't take a child for "Nutcracker" under seven years of age. He does hold open auditions each year, though he likes to use dancers from his school, if possible. "We train our students in a way so they can understand our director's and choreographer's needs," he says, and this, of course, makes it easier to teach them their roles.

For Bruce Wells, associate director of the Boston Ballet, matters are more straightforward. Since Boston is a large ballet company and has its own school of ballet, the auditioning process has natural limitations. "The children have to have studied at the Boston School of Ballet for at least one year," he says, before they are allowed to audition for "Nutcracker." "Seven years old is the earliest we will take them, and mainly they are eight years old and older."

At Boston, there are two days of auditions for "Nut-

A former "Clara" shows the steps and character needed at a "Nutcracker" audition.

Aspiring dancers perform steps during a "Nutcracker" audition.

cracker." The first day the students stay within their class, and their teachers — along with the artistic director and the balletmaster — gauge them not necessarily for the best technique but for being the best dancers. At the end of the day the students are given a color, depicting the group they will dance with (red for soldiers, green for angels, and so forth). Then, on the second day, the children return and audition with their particular color group. "At this point, I will make some eliminations," adds Wells, "mainly for overweight and height." As the day goes on he continues to pare down the numbers, "and by the end of the day I have the cast."

In Boston, all parts are triple cast because there will be forty-two performances. "That's a lot of performing for eight- to ten-year-olds," Wells admits.

What, though, do the artistic directors and balletmasters/ mistresses look for in the young dancers? Bruce Wells mentions not being overweight, but there is more. "The children have to have a certain style," believes Madeline Cantrella Culpo. "They have to have very nice feet for their low, intermediate level of training. They should have a look — childhood innocence — because "Nutcracker" is, after all, a period piece. The children should be graceful, and it helps if they have long hair."

Or as Francia Russell, artistic director of the Pacific Northwest Ballet Company in Seattle, put it: "We look for good bodies. We love long legs, a compatibility with our company style, a facility to pick up combinations, and a good attitude."

The "Nutcracker" experience carries with it the unfortunate consequences of rejection. Not everyone can have the role they wish; not everyone can perform to an artistic director's satisfaction. For a young dancer — even those as young as six or seven — the reality of rejection has to be faced. For some it will be a first experience, and every artistic director has seen the sad faces, tear-filled eyes, lips quivering, as someone else gets a coveted role. For the young dancer, the most sought-after role in "Nutcracker" is that of Clara, the child who shows concern for a broken toy and is rewarded with a fantastic dream, and it is in the auditions that this role is filled. "Clara embodies the spirit of Christmas," says Bruce Wells. "She is most likely to be the child who can act, rather than the one with incredible technique. She must emanate a youthful innocence. We find it is rare that children can perform this part two years in a row."

Rejection, however, sits over each of the dancers, whether they seek the role of Clara or someone else. "I think people and companies are more conscious of softening the experience of rejection now than in years past," adds Wells. "We talk about it with the kids and with their parents. We let the kids watch the methods of selection, and we try not to keep secrets. We make them part of the overall process."

The rejection problem seems easier, somehow, with the youngest children. They come to understand that they will have their chance "next year" or the year after that. They know they are the youngest and everyone will have their turn. It's the next age group, eight- to ten-year-olds, children Madeline Cantrella Culpo calls the "in-between" dancers where the problems could arise. She's gentle with them, explaining that not everyone can be in the roles, that there are other parts and they should consider trying out for those. "We try to talk to them honestly, make them realize this is an important experience, point out that we don't win everything we do." Then she laughs as she remembers a recent conversation with two other dance teachers. They were discussing their own daughters and the "Nutcracker" experience. "Not one of them ever danced Clara," she says, "not one. But they survived just fine."

Parents, unfortunately, can get caught up in the rejection situation, and it usually spells difficulty for the student, as well as for the relationship between student, parent and dance teacher. What the parents see, and what the artistic director sees, may be two entirely different things when it comes to auditioning, and it's best if the parents stay far away — out of sight and mind — from the actual audition. Most artistic directors, in fact, keep their auditions closed in order to avoid unhappy consequences. Basically, of course, parents and their children are interested in just one thing — why didn't the child get the role he/she auditioned for? — and certainly any reasonably competent artistic director would provide an appropriate answer. In the great majority of cases this suffices, but once in a while there is a parent who cannot or will not leave it alone. The consequences can be rather severe.

Madeline Cantrella Culpo remembers such a situation. She had a student who danced Clara one year, but had outgrown the role by the next year, though she hadn't outgrown her desire to do the role. "The mother tried to live her life through the daughter — Mom had wanted to be a dancer, but the daughter was not blessed with a dancer's body — and whenever the daughter did not get a part, the mother would come to me and try to force me to change my decision for her daughter." This went on for years, and the daughter continued to be the pawn of her mother's ambition.

Now, years later, the daughter is in her late teens. "She's suffering deep psychological distress; she has a lot of problems. She's not a dancer, and she will never be a dancer."

And that one role of Clara was probably the highlight of her dancer's experience ... as well as a millstone she still hasn't been able to throw off.

Parents feel bad when their child is disappointed, when they see the tears in the child's eyes. They want to make it better, but they should realize that disappointment is a part of life, that it's perfectly normal not to win everytime. The young mind is emotionally elastic, and a momentary disappointment will often be replaced with some other interest — even a success — before very long. One dance teacher tells of a little girl who has appeared at "Nutcracker" auditions for four years in a row without ever getting a part — until finally she's chosen to become an angel. "She looked at it as a challenge to keep going," the teacher says, "not as an insurmountable rejection. Her mother never said a word about it during those four years, and the little girl is as happy as she can be now."

Equal to "Nutcracker" auditions in importance and availability for young dancers are opportunities in various summer ballet programs. In substance and form, auditions for summer programs differ substantially from "Nutcracker" auditions, but they do represent another experience for the young dancer, one that should be utilized, if possible. It is the *experience* of auditioning that prepares the young dancer for the more serious demands of ballet performing in later years.

The summer programs usually run from three to six weeks and are an intensive ballet schooling that combines daily classes with regular performance (more about this in a later section). Generally, auditions (which are actual one- to two-hour classes) are held for the summer programs between January and March each year (local ballet teachers can provide information about the individual programs). The auditions are held in a number of towns and cities throughout the country by the artistic director or school director of the particular ballet company sponsoring the summer program. For Burklyn Ballet Theatre, for example, auditions are held in nineteen cities, coast to coast, and it can be a grueling schedule.

The first thing to note is that the children will probably

not be familiar with the person conducting the audition. They will be less comfortable, certainly more nervous, and parents should recognize the signs. But the artistic director or school director has definite needs in mind: "I look for actual ballet technique and talent," says Bruce Wells. "Three things stand out for me — no overweight, good proportion and nice flow of movement."

"We love a good attitude," adds Francia Russell of the Pacific Northwest Ballet Company. "We want our students to have a good and productive six weeks with us."

Attitude is certainly an important consideration:

Years ago I arrived to give an audition in a major Eastern city and the director told me with embarrassment that he had forgotten — a well-known master teacher was also due to give a class at the same time as my audition. Would I mind if my audition was combined with her class? I could watch her and audition the dancers that way? I had no problem with that because the master teacher was trained the same way as I was, so the class was bound to be similar to what I would give.

I only had interest in three of the twenty-five dancers in the class, and afterwards, I awarded a partial scholarship to one, and no scholarships to the others. Four weeks later, I got a nasty letter from one of those who didn't get a scholarship — I had been unfair. Why didn't I teach the class? How could I make these decisions when I didn't teach the class? I didn't bother to answer the letter because there was no point in debating my professional qualifications with someone who wouldn't have understood.

But the following year at my auditions in the same city, there was the girl who had written the nasty letter. She pushed her way to the front of the class until I acknowledged her by name. Her face fell because she didn't think I'd remember her letter. In the end, she never did get her scholarship — first, because the competition was quite stiff and she simply didn't measure up, and second, because she had the makings of a troublemaker and I wasn't about to award scholarship money to someone like that.

Audition classes for the summer programs can be quite

large. Usually, each dancer is assigned a number and the number is then matched to the application blank to attend the particular program. These are regular classes to the greatest possible degree, and the dancers are asked to do barre and centre work. From this the auditioner can get a good feel, not only for the young dancer's technique and training, but also his/her ability to learn combinations and choreography quickly.

Certainly it's important to take these audition classes, even if there is no present intention to become part of the summer program. The experience is essential — but the person conducting the audition should give some approval under these circumstances. The reason? The classes could become overcrowded otherwise. "I don't appreciate dancers taking my audition classes with no intent of coming to the summer program," says Francia Russell, "unless they ask me first. Usually I won't object."

For the young dancer, auditioning is experience. In the past few years some summer programs have instituted a small charge for the audition to defray travel and other expenses. It's a nominal amount, really, but it also serves to emphasize that auditioning is a learning process, too, and for the young dancer that's the key to better technique.

Part V:

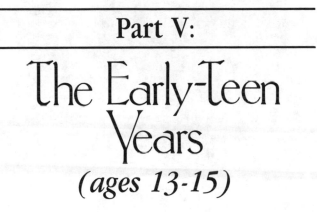

The Early-Teen Years
(ages 13-15)

An obsession with dancing and performing is quite normal.

—————————Chapter 1:—————————
Lifestyle of the Teenaged Dancer

While other parents contend with the blasting cacophony of the current rage in rock groups, a young dancer's parents will hear the strains of Tchaikovsky, Stravinsky, Vivaldi . . . over and over, loud to be sure, but the lilt and the complexity of the music will carry compensations.

No ear-splitting, twanging guitars, no heart-thumping, staccato drum beats, no non-melodic refrains.

Of course, the young dancer will be dancing throughout the house, improvising ballets, rehearsing steps learned for an upcoming performance. Twirling, jumping . . . flailing legs, soaring arms . . . balancing a ballet foot on a recently cleaned kitchen counter. "I'm just stretching. Dancers have to stretch!" . . . high kicking in the dining room. "You just missed grandmother's china!" . . .

The teenaged dancer lives, eats and breathes dance. It is an obsession that quickly rises to excess. But this is not all bad. If the young dancer has any career aspirations in the dance field, it's best to face it now. Dance is a way of life, it is a demanding and encompassing life choice, and even teenagers in their single-minded obsessions can begin to grasp what will be required.

In the morning, right out of bed, the young dancer will do thirty-forty minutes of stretching exercises, limbering up from the stiffness of a night's sound sleep. There may have been a late rehearsal the evening before, so unfinished homework must be faced. On the bedroom walls are posters or photos of the ballet superstars — Mikhail Barishnykov, Peter Martins, Fernando Bujones, Alessandra Ferri, Judith Fugate . . . role models, all. Pointe shoes litter the floor, some with ribbons severed or shanks pulled out, no longer usable. Sodden balls of lambs wool fill the basket and bottles of floor wax shellac share a table with polyurethane floor sealer and tubes and jars of theatrical make-up. Blue rubber foot strengtheners lie on the bed admist a pile of mutilated clothing . . . "What did you *do* to that pretty leotard I bought you last month!" The back's been cut and the front is safety pinned, full-length parachute pants have been cut into shorts.

"It lets me dance better."

There's more. Tights have their feet and crotch cut out.

"So I can wear them on my arms under a leotard," is the ready answer.

Other tights have their foot bottom seams cut open.

"So I can fix up my feet if they bleed or blister."

In stark witness are bandage wrappers strewn about, some already opened.

And then there is the ballet bag. Made of lightweight, waterproof nylon, it carries *everything!* Sweaty leotards, floor wax, deodorant, hairspray, crumbled cookies, stale apples . . . dig a little deeper and there's more: four or five pairs of pointe shoes (none in working shape), a couple of ratty-looking chiffon skirts, at least two pair of flat ballet slippers, numerous pink and black tights, bobby pins, combs . . .

Everything.

Ballet bag over a shoulder, homework under an arm, the young dancer now appears at the breakfast table. And here's where a parent's major responsibility comes in. In growing a fine dancer, a parent must insure that the young dancer eats correctly, that a strong and healthy body is achieved. A dancer's body is his/her instrument, it must be kept at an optimum weight, strong growth without excess fat is crucial. This, of course, means that fast-food grazing and teen-diet crazes must be guarded against; that a balanced meal program is followed.

It's not easy. "If teenage dancers would only care as much about what they put *in* their bodies as they care about what they put *on* their bodies, we would have a much stronger performer," says Jeraldyne Blunden of the Dayton (Ohio) Contemporary Dance Company. She has eleven young people in a junior company, and they perform regularly throughout the year. Physically, it is a grueling schedule — especially when it is mixed with school requirements and other teenaged social demands. The dancers must keep their bodies well-tuned. "I tell them that if they were musicians and playing a Stradivarious violin, they would polish it and polish it. They would care for it completely and never let me touch it," she says, understanding, of course, that to demand such perfection from teenagers is highly unrealistic. But she tries. "They don't understand they have only one body in one life." She laughs. "They wear Yves St. Laurent and eat at McDonald's."

Because dancers spend so much time in physical activities, many parents find it important to see if they can have their young people excluded from physical education classes in school. Many schools will go along and schedule free periods during physical education time, or they will allow the young dancer to leave school early in order to attend ballet class.

But suppose a school doesn't want to — or can't — allow students to miss physical education classes? For the parent, the first step is to investigate state education laws: Are there provisions for talented young people who wish to pursue a professional career immediately after high school? Some states have laws like this and they provide that training during the school day or training which duplicates school training and which leads to a professional career can be followed and can excuse the young person from certain school requirements.

Understand the ballet demands on the young dancer — one and one-half hours of ballet class per day, a class in variations, modern dance, partnering, jazz dancing and character dancing once a week, two or three pointe classes per week. Many good ballet schools require their students to take classes in French, music notation and history of dance each week...

All in all, a minimum of three hours per day, five days per week.

And if the young dancer is also in rehearsal, a member of a junior or regional company, add another four to eight hours per week, plus some additional time as the performance date approaches.

Performing — it's what every young dancer wants to do. Young dancers exist to perform, though sometimes such a narrow focus can miss other valuable aspects of the ballet world:

> *I was fifteen years old and a committed ballet dancer. I had left Canada with my parents' blessings and boarded a ship bound for England where I would continue my ballet studies. My vision was clear — in a few short years, I would become the toast of Europe, a ballerina with such grace and delicate movement that major companies would bid for my services.*
>
> *One day, as the ship plied its way across the Atlantic, I took a seat on deck and immediately noticed a woman wearing ballet shoes.*
>
> *"You must be a dancer," I said.*
>
> *She shook her head. "I'm a Laban Notator."*
>
> *I had heard of Rudolph Von Laban, of course. His work had been the major source of ballet choreography recording in all the years before film and video tape. His techniques provided a history of ballet choreography, and the system was invaluable, especially for restoring important ballets.*
>
> *But I was fifteen, and I was interested in performing!*
>
> *"Would you like to learn Notation?" the woman asked.*
>
> *"Thank you," I said politely, "but I want to dance. I'm a performer, really."*
>
> *Later, I found out the woman was a primary disciple of Rudolph Von Laban in America, and in the week we had been on the ship, she could have taught me much that I needed to know about the essential skills in choreography notation...*

An obsession with dancing and performing, then, is quite normal with a younger dancer. If that obsession can be expanded to include other — less exciting — aspects of the field, the young dancer benefits greatly. Knowledge of the history and the traditions of ballet are important for a full appreciation of the art form, and in the end even the dancer will come to dance better.

Of course, try and tell that to a glamour-obsessed fourteen-year-old.

The truth often hovers about the young dancer, and in time they come to appreciate it. The teenager faced with drugs, sex and alcohol, with peer pressure to conform, can find in ballet a world consumed with other things. "I never had the temptation to be 'normal' " says a young professional dancer of twenty, who remembers what it was like to be in her early teens. My body was — and is — too important an instrument to try putting drugs and alcohol into it."

The life style, then, of the young teenaged dancer is one of obsession and time contraint. There simply will never be enough time to do the things that friends and peers are doing, unless they, too, are dancers. Homework, school attendance, social life, will be greatly influenced by the demands of a dance schedule, and through it all the young dancer must maintain a healthy body and a sound outlook. It may seem as if dance has taken priority over every aspect of a young teenager's life, that nothing else will matter.

But in reality, dance is simply one type of teenaged obsession, as with computer technology or rock music or pumping iron. The career demands of ballet may require utter dedication, but to the young dancer there is nothing unusual about this.

For in the end, the young dancer is a teenager before he or she is a dancer.

The joy of performance is the ultimate reward.

Chapter 2:
Performing Arts Schools

Lydia Joel tells a story. "I remember talking with a teacher from Oregon who taught a literature course. Every April she had her students do an essay on 'spring', and the results were fairly predictable. 'The flowers are growing'... 'The sun is shining'... Nothing creative or new. But one year something surprising happened. The music teacher and the math teacher required the students to look at spring from their perspectives — how the wind blows, what it sounds like, how things grow, what's the musical interpretation? Suddenly the essays on spring became vividly innovative, each completely different. One set a scene on top of the Empire State Building, another in a cave face to face with a dinosaur."

These are essays on spring?

"The point is that the students were unburdened from rote thinking. They were allowed to discover the limits of their literary selves."

Lydia Joel is former head of dance at the New York City High School for the Performing Arts — site of the movie, "Fame," and its television counterpart — and she sees the performing arts school as the dance equivalent of literary exploration. "If a young person is interested in ballet as a career, it is far preferable to attend a performing arts school because dance and academics are taught side by side. One interrelates with the other. The creative approach brings out the responsiveness in all kids."

The performing arts school is of recent vintage in this country. Unlike its cousin, the dance company school of ballet, the performing arts school was developed as a place where *all* the performing arts — music, theatre, as well as dance — could be learned. It was a place where young people with talent could remain at home and find proper instruction and performing outlets while maintaining sufficient academic discipline.

The New York City High School of Performing Arts, developed in the late 1940s, was the first of its kind. Famed singer-dancer-performer Eartha Kitt, in fact, was a member of the first class, and "right from the beginning," according to Lydia Joel, "the thing clicked like crazy." In succeeding years, other performing arts schools have sprung up such as the Chicago Academy of the Arts, the Performing Arts School of Philadelphia, the Los Angeles County High School of the Arts, the School for Creative and Performing Arts in Cincinnati, Ohio, all offering integrated dance instruction with academics, emphasizing and re-emphasizing career orientation.

As with any other high school, the performing arts schools are available to anyone residing in the community. Generally, however, auditions are required because places in each class are limited — two-hundred, for example, in the four upper grades at the New York City High School of the Performing Arts. Something more than desire, therefore, is required to get in.

But not necessarily prior dance training.

"What we looked for was a glow," says Lydia Joel, "a radiance, a sense of excitement and space, a presence. It's nice if it turns out to be someone who has had beautiful training, who has beautiful arches, and a gorgeous body."

But it's not required. "We wanted to see potential, something special."

And, of course, that translates into very individual judgment.

The performing arts school day is roughly divided into two parts — studio and academics. Half the day is spent with one area, half with the other, though individual schools may put a little more emphasis in one segment or the other. There are no library periods, rest periods or physical education periods, but the students may be exposed to dance history and special character dance in order to broaden their horizons. The point of it all is simple — can the regular high school routine be restructured so that talented youngsters may pursue dance training — and ultimately a dance career — while simultaneously carrying on with academic requirements in the same place and at the same time?

After more than forty years, the answer has to be a resounding yes!

But what of the young dancer who seeks a dance career through one of the schools of a recognized ballet company? How different can it be from attending a performing arts high school?

Actually, going to a company ballet school is the accepted procedure in most of Europe as well as in Russia. A child is auditioned at ten years old and those that pass the audition are accepted into professional training schools where they complete their ballet and high school academics training simultaneously. In Russia, for example, these young people graduate into the Kirov and Bolshoi Ballet companies; in England, they move into the Royal Ballet or the Festival Ballet Company.

In the United States, the closest training approach to the Russian or European models is the School of American Ballet (known as SAB) in New York City. It was started in the 1950s by George Balanchine and Lincoln Kirsten, and its graduates are groomed for the New York City Ballet Company (though not everyone is accepted). It is probably the finest training ground for the truly "American dancer", and over the years it has prepared dancers for careers, not only with the New York City Ballet, but with every major ballet company in the western world.

"First, we must have a school," is the famous phrase uttered by George Balanchine, when the idea of a New York City Ballet Company was proposed many years ago. What he meant was that a ballet company could live best if it had a school to provide it with a continual flow of dancers who had learned *his* way, *his* technique. The school was — and is — the key.

But unlike schools such as the Kirov or the Royal Ballet, the School of American Ballet is not state-supported. Everything is privately organized from funding to repertoire to performance schedule. SAB is a private ballet school. There are no academics, no high school classes.

So the concentration on ballet is even more severe. Acceptance is by audition, of course, and students apply from across the country. "What we look for first is the potential for training that body," says Robert Lindgren, director of SAB. "Good feet, high arches, limberness, general facility to kick the legs high, a good proportion to the shoulders and the hips, length of neck, size of head . . . these are what we judge in the beginner."

And if the young dancer has had training? "We look to see whether they are rolling their feet, whether they know the vocabulary, whether they do a decent fifth position, a decent plie, a decent grand battement, a decent pirouette . . ."

Lindgren has been working with young dancers for many years, soon after he gave up his own ballet career with Ballet Russe de Monte Carlo. There is one essential he seeks: "We look for attractive people; we look for that sense of coordination and musicality."

Some young people, he knows, simply don't have these things.

But if the young dancer is accepted into SAB, a whole new world beckons. The earliest age for acceptance is eight, and students can expect to take two classes per week. By the time they are sixteen or seventeen, they will be taking ten classes per week.

During the early years, some children get a chance to audition for, and dance with, the New York City Ballet performances of "Nutcracker." And should the company require children in any of its other performances, the first place they look is SAB.

After years of training — which might include several sessions at SAB's summer school — between thirty to forty dancers make it to the highest level (known as level D). From this group the dancers are chosen for the end of year "workshop" which is attended by dance critics and company directors from all over the country. It is these dancers who have the best chance of getting a contract with a professional company, and it is from here, of course, that the New York City Ballet is able to pick its new company members.

Two things must be understood about SAB: it offers no residence accommodations, it offers no academic training. It offers ballet training, it offers dance classes, it offers performance. That is all.

Where, then, do young people from out of town live while attending SAB? There is no easy answer, though there are plans to erect an SAB dormitory which would eventually house some students. Becky Metzger, a young dancer from Atlanta, Georgia, was accepted into SAB at age fifteen and is now a member of the New York City Ballet Company. Her reaction is typical. "The living situation was the most difficult problem to overcome when I first

At a performing arts school, dance and academics are taught side by side.

came to New York," she says. "The school helped me get a place, but that didn't work out well. I had difficulties with the people I was living with, and it just wasn't a very good year."

Some out-of-town SAB students choose to live at the YMCA or YWCA; others are fortunate to find a host family or to be helped by SAB itself, as was Becky Metzger. Occasionally, entire families decide to move to New York so their dancing child can study at SAB; others split up with one parent moving to New York with the child. No wonderful options here, but for these parents it is preferable to allowing a teenager the run of New York City without supervision.

Then, there's still the matter of academics. A teenager needs academics. For many the answer is the New York Professional Children's School, a private high school directly responsive to the time constraints and career orientations of the young dancer. Actually, the student population consists of young actors, musicians, dancers and models, all of whom must mix training and performing with academic classroom time. "PCS is different from a regular high school," says Becky Metzger, who attended for several years. "In my Atlanta high school they didn't understand about performing requirements." The fact that she might not have been able to do a paper because she had classes and rehearsals until ten p.m. meant nothing. But at PCS it does. "The teachers are really supportive — it's small, maybe seven to ten in a class, and the school goes all the way through the twelfth grade."

What's important for the young dancer is this: the school allows generous release time to attend dance classes, rehearsals, filmings and photo sessions. Students arrange their school schedules to fit their career needs.

For young dancers who prefer to be trained outside New York City and yet wish to live away from home, there is the North Carolina School of the Performing Arts in Winston-Salem, North Carolina. It is the only national school devoted exclusively to the performing arts, and its students live and train on the campus. The school gives the dancer a well-rounded education in all the arts with an emphasis, of course, on dance. It is state supported and designed, according to Robert Lindgren, who headed the dance department for many years, "to attract talented, young people from twelve years of age and offer an arts education and an academic education in supervised dormitories through high school graduation."

Dance opportunities abound. There is an annual "Nutcracker" performance as well as other performances throughout the year in the school's fine theatre. And sometimes dance tours of the state are arranged.

NCSA, however, differs from pure ballet schools such as SAB. It is looking to train dancers as well as other performing artists, and its approach is more general. "We were training for the field of dance and not specifically for ballet," says Robert Lindegren. "We took students who had the potential to be dancers but also the potential to be theatrical people — we did ballet and modern side-by-side."

A wider exposure for the dancer, a greater level of exposure. "It is," says Lindgren, "the only school of its kind in America."

What about away-from-home schools that offer dance training on a par with an overall generalized academic curriculum? The so-called "prep" school. Two might be considered:

— *Walnut Hill School,* Natick, Massachusetts. The program was started in the early 1970s by Sydelle Gomberg for students in the seventh through twelfth grades. Dancers are accepted into a ballet or modern dance major after an audition, and they take a minimum of two dance classes per day while maintaining a regular academic schedule. A close working relationship with the Boston Ballet creates special opportunities for instruction and performance.

— *St. Paul's School,* Concord, New Hampshire. Richard Rein, formerly with the American Ballet Theatre, started a dance program here in the late 1970s. There is a separate building solely for dance, with huge, airy studios and several fine performing spaces. The school's emphasis is more on academics than on the arts, so a young dancer seeking acceptance must satisfy the academic requirements first. An audition is required.

My child wants more dance training, the parent of a young teenager will utter, knowing only that classes once or twice a week at the local studio are unsatisfying. There are other choices:

— is a local performing arts high school available?

— what about a local company ballet school?

— what about moving to a locale where ballet opportunities abound?

— what about a boarding school in the performing arts or with a strong dance program?

The high school years are crucial for the young dancer. This is when the craft of ballet is honed or discarded. This is also where a firm grasp of academics will or will not be attained. The parent who searches both avenues and develops good opportunity for the young dancer is the parent who can truly be said to have made an unparalleled contribution to a budding career.

My child, the dancer. The parent can smile.

Dancers are constantly aware of their bodies.

─────────*Chapter 3:*─────────
Proper Weight and Improper Habits

Too fat! Too fat! Too fat! ... The young dancer's lament.
   "I wish you'd eat better," an army of concerned mothers say, ruefully acknowledging an uphill battle. "You *need* your strength."
   "I feel fine."
   "At your age you should have a healthy diet. You are still growing."
   "Oh, Mother!"
   "Look at what you eat — diet soda through the day, junk food and candy bars. Is that a healthy diet?"
   "I've got to keep my weight down."
   "Nonsense! You are still a growing child ..."
   So it goes. Legions of mothers and legions of young dancers have played this scene with appropriate variations through the years. The young dancer thinks she is too fat, the mother thinks she is neglecting her health in order to push her weight down.
   The point with young dancers is this: they all — *all* — think they are too heavy, they all think they must lose weight in order to dance effectively and present the most perfect body form. Weight loss, they think, is a magic key to ballet success.
   Nothing could be further from the truth. Obviously,

weight *control* — not weight loss — is crucial for a dancer. Grace and beauty are more effectively portrayed by a slim body than by a chubby one, but that doesn't mean a young dancer must strive to be lean at the expense of health and artistic expression.

Listen to what happened to a young member of a highly lauded international company. The mother tells the story: "The artistic director recently choreographed a new 'Nutcracker' and gave the solo role of Snow Queen to my daughter. She was thrilled and determined to lose some weight before opening night — though the artistic director never suggested it — even though she was slender enough anyway. Ten pounds and a few weeks later, she had lost her strength and her muscle sense . . . and a month before opening night she lost the part.

"But I guess she learned a lesson. After the tears and the self-recriminations, she made up her mind to regain the part. Through careful and healthy eating, and with the loving concern and attention of the company's prima ballerina, she put on enough weight so the artistic director allowed her to dance the part after all. And, in fact, she danced the part throughout the entire 'Nutcracker' season."

A happy ending. But it almost wasn't.

Is there a proper weight for ballet? Bodies come in all shapes and sizes and types. The perfect dancing weight for a five-foot-seven-inch dancer can be as low as one-hundred-five pounds and as high as one-hundred-thirty; and for a five-foot-two-inch dancer the proper weight can vary from ninety to one-hundred-ten pounds. Body structure, muscle development, even bone size make the difference, and there simply isn't one answer for everyone.

That doesn't mean, of course, that young dancers won't think otherwise. In this — as in so many aspects of a dancer's training — the parent's role is to provide some form of equilibrium, some sanity to the young dancer's obsessive quest for pound shedding.

"Why not drink fruit juice?"

"Calories, Mom. This is better." A can of diet soda within reach.

"V-8™, tomato juice, orange juice, any of them would be healthier."

"I feel fine."

What's happening is that the body is seeking liquid to quench the loss of fluid from sweat after physical exertion. Diet soda will accomplish this but it adds nothing to the nutritional demands that have also built up. The young dancer thinks that diet soda and perspiration are a trade-off... but that is not the case. When a dancer sweats, more than water escapes — there are nutrients such as potassium and sodium that must be replaced.

A fruit juice, even a low-caloried fruit juice, will help more than a can of diet soda.

"Weight is *my* problem!" the young dancer will insist.

"Your *health* is my concern!" the parent should respond.

"Maybe I'll start smoking, then."...

Another bad habit for the parent to deal with. Dancers through the years have used smoking as a means of weight control, knowing that it supresses the appetite. But there's always the risk that the cure will be worse than the disease. It's got a double-barreled effect on the dancer: first, smoking will cut into the dancer's wind, and this could influence stamina and strength, especially during extensive rehearsals and performances; second, it adds no nutritional benefit to replace the loss of weight the dancer seeks. Pounds come off, perhaps, and with them whatever strength and physical development they represent.

People smoke for many reasons, and this book is no place to debate the morality of the habit. But parents should be on the lookout for one thing... does a young dancer use smoking as a way to control and/or lose weight? If so, then the parent should encourage some healthy, nutritional substitute so that whatever strength and stamina is lost can be replaced.

"Maybe I won't smoke after all."

"Your body is beautiful just the way it is, dear."

Concern about weight remains important not only with dancers but also with school directors. Precise weight levels, however, are rarely followed. It is more a case of sensing significant change, noting that a dancer "looks different" or dances differently. At the School of American Ballet, for example, director Robert Lindgren says, "We don't weigh our students in here — we deal with weight problems in an informal manner. The teachers are always on the lookout for either weight gain or weight loss, and they will mention it right away if they see it." For Lindgren and other teachers, the underlying concern is that the young dancer will panic about a sudden weight gain and go on a crash diet which might have more permanent physical side effects. Many of these young people are moving from puberty into maturity. Their bodies are undergoing change even without dietary pressure. "The hardest thing is gaining energy," says Lindgren, and as the young dancer's body grows, the last thing she should do is expend whatever energy she has by severe dieting. "Most of the time the dancers put themselves through the agony of dieting because everyone else looks thin so they want this too," yet they overlook the fact that they may be robbing their own natural growth patterns. "So we ask whether the weight loss is something caused by diet or by something the dancer can't help," and if it's diet-based, other solutions may be sought.

One possible approach is that followed by the school of the Hartford Ballet in Connecticut. Enid Lynn, director of the school, says that while they talk about proper weight, they avoid putting a great deal of emphasis on it. "We don't weigh students in, we've never done that. They know if they're overweight, all they have to do is look in the mirror. We also make it known to them that certain roles will not be available if their weight is too high." If they are too thin, however, outside help is beckoned. "We talk to those we think are having trouble, and we recommend they get counseling. We know who to send them to, though we don't ride herd on them." Therapists familiar with anorexia, bulimia and other eating disorders are available, though the therapy is a family-oriented type of thing. The therapists, in fact, won't see the young dancer unless the family consents to come, too. The parents must see this not as a disease the young dancer picked from the air like a common cold, but as something with roots that stretched back into early childhood.

"We always talk directly to the parents," Enid Lynn says, "but some don't recognize the weight loss problems their children have. We, after all, see the young dancers undressed, so we know what's happening." Some parents, unfortunately, won't agree to participate in the counseling, so the kids don't get treated.

"That," she adds, "is the saddest part."

And then there is the story of Leah who fought the weight battle, not foolishly nor unwisely, but without realizing her dream. Leah's mother was pretty and pleasant . . . and quite round. Her father was tall and lean. Both parents supported Leah's obsession to become a ballet dancer, and by age fourteen she was a strong, well-proportioned performer. Everyone was pleased and looking forward to an exciting future.

Then Leah became sixteen, and almost overnight she became too heavy for professional ballet work. She had moved from puberty into early maturity, and her body had grown up. She tried to diet, she went to a nutritionist . . . and finally she lost the un-

Proper weight permits the body to perform in its most graceful manner.

wanted pounds, but under very controlled circumstances.

An audition followed, and on a happy, happy day she was offered a scholarship apprenticeship with a major ballet company!

The future was exciting again.

But only briefly. Once she was away from the nutritionist and out of her controlled environment, the weight began to come back. Inexorably it returned, and after six difficult months, she faced the shattering of her dream. She realized she had inherited her mother's body configuration — not her father's — and she would never become a skinny ballerina.

Unless she wanted to starve herself through the rest of her dance career. She had talent, she had excellent training, but the price for ultimate success was simply too high.

And so she turned to other things.

Proper weight, then, is not — and should not be — a goal in itself. It is a means to permit the body to perform in its most graceful, most sublime manner. Any young dancer who thinks of losing weight as the unlocking of a magic door to ballet success is bound for disappointment and heartache.

At regional festivals, young dancers have a chance to perform in a professional atmosphere.

Chapter 4:
The Regional Ballet Experience

"Regional dance exposed me to the professional side of the art," says a young American dancer now with a major Canadian ballet company. She remembers her early teen years. "I met and studied with people like Robert Joffrey of the American School of Ballet, Barbara Weisberger of the Pennsylvania Ballet, Virginia Williams of the Boston Ballet. I think I learned more about professional auditions in one forty-five minute seminar with Richard Englund (of the American Ballet Theatre) than anywhere else."

This is the essence of regional ballet, an opportunity for the young dancer to test the waters of semi-professional ballet. Its public face is the annual festival where regional ballet companies come together for training, seminars and performances, and it is here that the young dancer can savor the fruits of grueling hours at the barre and late night rehearsals.

Its other face is the regional dance company which provides high-quality community offerings for young dancers to refine their art and to learn what it's like to be a part of a dance team. Regional dance companies exist in most parts of the country, and they perform on a regular basis throughout the year. Ballet teachers are aware of the regional company most appropriate and most convenient to their school. They can certainly offer recommendations and set up auditions. The important thing is to realize that these opportunities exist, and that young dancers should be encouraged to take advantage of them.

Dancers can become members of a regional ballet company at the age of thirteen, and frequently, they continue with the company right through high school, until they enter college or go off to a fully professional career. For the young dancer this means a commitment beyond what they have experienced up to now; it means they have become part of a close-knit group that will rely upon them to perform consistently and regularly. "We usually ask our young dancers to sign a 'moral' contract when they first join us," says Maxine Chapman, artistic director of the Vineland (New Jersey) Dance Company. "It isn't that we will take them to court if they break it, but that they understand they have agreed to a commitment, not only for themselves but to all the other dancers in the company."

No way is this an empty exercise, either. Chapman's company does twenty to thirty performances per year, offering both ballet and theatre dancing (as seen in such musicals as "Cats"). "Our proximity to Atlantic City has given us the chance to get some of our dancers into shows and to perform on television."

A dancer joining a regional dance company must agree to make a one-year commitment to attend classes, rehearsals and performances. This is only fair because company plans and programs are often set up at least one year in advance, and in order to cast ballet roles, the artistic director will need to know who will be available. It also represents the type of commitment professional ballet dancers assume, and, if nothing else, the regional company is a training ground for that elusive eventuality.

The regional ballet company year comprises — roughly — four definite parts. The young company member participates in all of them. There are:

— ballet *technique* classes held about three-hundred days per year.

— rehearsals and performances for "Nutcracker" which occur October through December.

— rehearsals from February through April for the spring performance at home and at the regional ballet festival.

— summer training classes at the National Choreographic Conference or summer ballet programs in July and August.

It's a big commitment for young dancers, and it should not be lightly entered into. The average schedule includes a minimum of three one and one-half hour classes during the week, as well as four to eight hours of rehearsals during the weekend, usually on Sundays. Since we're dealing with young teenagers, we have to be aware that this schedule, coupled with the normal ballet class schedule, can become burdensome unless the unabashed commitment is made. The young dancers have to know that during these years at least, dance will be the major focus of their physical lives. Anything less than a full commitment can only be destructive to the dancer, his or her parents, and, ultimately, the dancer's company.

For the conscientious young dancer, however, the regional dance company can mean a permanent uplift in the dance experience.

For Mom and Dad, it could mean that Sundays, Thanksgiving and the Christmas holiday season might be spent in a different manner, perhaps even a different location, than expected.

"The show must go on," the young dancer will offer without apology.

"Whatever happened to the holidays?" Mom and Dad will ask themselves.

"I love to dance," will be the reply.

Most regional dance companies are members of the National Association of Regional Ballets, and each year there are festivals that bring together these companies. The festivals are the highlight of the regional company year. They occur in several areas of the country corresponding to appropriate geographic areas. There are, for example, the Northeast, the Southeast, the Mid-States Associations, and so forth. As many as twenty-five to thirty regional dance companies appear at a festival, and the air is filled with teenaged excitement, dance and performance opportunity. "Festivals serve to let the dancers see that there are kids from all over the country putting in the same commitment they are required to put in," says Jeraldyne Blunden of the Dayton Contemporary Dance Company. She has been taking her regional ballet company to festivals for fifteen years. All the dancers go, even those who may not be performing. It's important for her

Regional ballet company experiences create lasting friendships.

dancers to see that a multitude of others share their interest, that they are not alone. "It's hard for young dancers, in their daily lives, to withstand peer pressure from friends who aren't into danc-ing... "you've got to dance *again* tonight... why?... Jeraldyne Blunden shows them they have other peers who *do* understand.

There's a lot more to gain from these festivals than young dancers seeking support from other young dancers, of course. Maxine Chapman describes some of them: "The dancers get a chance to work with other dancers in master classes, to perform on a national level with youngsters of the same age and to grow by watching other companies." It's peer learning carried out of the school room and into the dance world, and it works well. It can broaden a young dancer immeasurably. "Many of the 'strictly classical company' dancers get their first glimpse of modern works at the festival performances," adds Chapman, indicating the wide sweep of performance opportunity at the festivals.

There's more, though. The festival performances are a showcase for the young dancers. Summer program directors, as well as professional company directors, often attend, and if they see what they like, they will offer scholarships, apprenticeships and even company contracts. "It's difficult to find this many young people in one place at one time all involved with the same thing," says the artistic director of a small professional company in New England. "We can usually find high-quality dancers whenever we need them."

Another aspect of regional ballet opportunity is the Craft of Choreography Conference, also sponsored by the National Association of Regional Ballets. To Jeraldyne Blundin this can be a most important experience for the young dancer because "this is where she or he learns to step from the student dancer mentality to the professional idiom." As well as performing, the young dancer now learns the basics of choreography. The choreographers use the dancers to create new works, and the dancers are expected to perform everyday. "They don't necessarily work with members of their own company or with their own artistic director or choreographer." The conference runs for two weeks, and the students must do consistently high-quality work in class, in the rehearsal hall and, finally, on the performance stage every evening. Over and over until it's right, until it's no longer an amateur effort.

"I believe that consistency is the earmark of the professional," adds Blunden, and after two weeks of intensive work with various choreographers the students would probably agree.

Julie, a fourteen-year-old dancer, asked me if she could try her hand with choreography during our summer program. I was delighted, and along with two twelve-year-old friends, she produced a work that we performed at one of our weekly presentations. The two twelve-year-olds showed the work to their regional company director and it was included in the company's repertoire, but the company never attended festivals. Julie, on the other hand, took the work to her director and she encouraged her to expand it. The next year, Julie's new version was chosen by the Princeton (New Jersey) Ballet Company as its "Young Choreographers" Festival offering.

Five years later, the two twelve-year-olds (now seventeen), brought the work back to our summer program, and they too, had expanded upon it! But because they had not had Julie's experience with festivals and choreography training, their work was not nearly so dynamic. It still suffered from amateurism.

Not all young dancers intend to pursue a career in dance,

but that should not prevent them from seeking to become a part of a regional ballet company. As Maxine Chapman puts it, "Regional ballet is like one enormous family," and it can provide a young person with a full, active and healthy teenaged experience. "It's important that these young people get the chance to perform in large, well-equipped theatres and before well-educated, appreciative people."

"I love to dance," the young dancer will say again and again.

Maxine Chapman would nod. "The ballet experience is great for a teenager's self-esteem."

Jazz and modern dance expand a ballet dancers horizons.

————Chapter 5:————
Jazz and Modern Dancing

Picture this: the young dancer, age fourteen, six years of ballet training, classes two, three times per week, total dedication to the ballet art form ("There's so much to learn; a ballerina has to be perfect!")...

An audition is announced. *Young dancers needed for community-sponsored musical review...* The choreographer has Broadway credits, there will be payment and the possibility of further television work.

"Not for me," the young dancer says.

"It's dancing," her mother responds, perplexed.

"I dance ballet."

"Isn't it the same?"

"Oh, Mother! Ballet is art, the rest is just . . . toe tapping."

"Is that what your teachers say?"

The young dancer looks embarrassed. "Not really . . ."

"I think you should audition. Might be fun."

"It's not ballet." . . .

A conversation like this is not uncommon in a young dancer's home. In their early teens, young dancers get exposure to variations of dance that are often grouped under jazz and modern

117

technique (folk and character dance forms are also part of this). After years of classical ballet training, the young dancer is ready for some variety, and with pure ballet that is difficult to find. But an exposure to jazz and/or modern dance training can create renewed interest in all dance forms as well as provide a previously undiscovered creative avenue for the young dancer. It is, in effect, a major dividend from all those years of tightly organized ballet training.

Jazz and modern dance expand a ballet dancer's horizons because a number of options now become available. Even if the young dancer is just thirteen or fourteen years old, opportunities for performing in musical theatre, in television or movies, video or industrial productions are possible. A sound balletic training is the essential ingredient, and a young dancer with six to eight years of serious ballet work should have little difficulty performing the jazz and/or modern dance choreography that will be set out. Rochelle McReynolds of the Boston Ballet, started her career with ballet but in her teens she found jazz dancing more satisfying, and now it is her main concentration. "A large amount of work is available for jazz dancers," she says, "a lot of television work especially, if one pursues it. But dancers have to be willing to work in industrials, too. I made more money in industrials sometimes than I could ever get shooting a commercial. We were seen by people who would eventually provide money to sponsor other performances."

But she insists, "ballet is the basis," and the reasons are obvious. Ballet adds the clean line, the turn out and the extremely stretched foot so that line and arms are very clear in design. Unless the young dancer has that training, jazz and modern dance have little character to sustain themselves.

It really works this way. Take the story of Thelma who had been trained in a well-known middle western regional ballet company. She had beautiful ballet technique, and before she had finished high school, artistic directors from various companies were watching her with glee. She accepted a scholarship to prepare to join a major New York City company, and her ballet career seemed poised for success. Then, one day, she was offered a dance role in a video in Italy, and she accepted it. Within a short time she had given up her scholarship in New York and devoted herself to commercial and video work in Italy and elsewhere. It was not classical ballet work, *but* it was dancing! Two years later, Thelma was offered a part in the television series "Fame," and once her run on that show was finished, she decided to go to acting school to become a full time actress.

"She can do anything she wants," says the artistic director of that regional ballet company where she danced during her early teens. "From that base of classical ballet — which was her passion, by the way — she has really gone places."

And it probably wouldn't have happened without the ballet background.

Jazz and modern dance are often linked together, but actually they are quite different, and in their differences we can see their individualized appeal. "Modern dance tends to stay ethereal," says Rochelle McReynolds, "a bit more esoteric, while jazz tends to work from the gut — not that modern dance doesn't work from the gut, too — but it tends to be intellectual work from

Jazz dancers need the same pure line and extension as ballet dancers.

the gut, while jazz tends to be sensual work from gut." The pelvis is often the focus of work in jazz, while with modern dance the center of focus is more in the diaphram area, it is less involved with earthy representations. "Put it this way," Rochelle McReynolds says, "the thrust of jazz dancing is much more sexual-sensual, the thrust of modern dance is much more intellectual."

In jazz technique the dancer learns to isolate each part of the body and then learns to change focus. Ballet trains a dancer to work all the sections of the body together, and when the dancer deals with jazz technique, she/he is able to understand the body isolations ("The rib cage, the rib cage, it should point like an arrow!") and to apply these isolations to today's choreography. Eddy Toussaint, artistic director of Ballet de Montreal, describes the meld of ballet training and jazz application for his choreography this way: "... it is still with beauty of line, beauty of pointe work, beauty of jump ... but suddenly — *la!* — it is a jazz movement, something close to us, something the people can put in themselves."

Jazz dancing is us! It is earthy, it is basic, it is our physical selves in communication.

Not so with modern dancing. This truly American form of dance was started by Martha Graham, Ruth St. Denis and Ted Shawn, and it has little history beyond the past fifty years. There are many techniques, almost as many as people dancing them, and a wide variety of approaches. The key to modern dance is improvization, and in this it is far apart from classical ballet. Modern dance is an extremely personal approach, while classical ballet with its beginnings in the royal courts hundreds of years ago has a definite vocabulary that the centuries have solidified ... barre work, center floor, adagios, grand allegros ... Modern dance is not so constrained, there is a freer style, more emphasis on interpretation. As Ruth Ambrose of the Boston Conservatory says, "With classical ballet the emotion should fit the actual step, with modern dance the emotion makes the step."

Where, then, might one look for a good jazz or modern dance teacher?

No surprise. Start with a good ballet school. Ask if the school teaches jazz or modern. If not, ask for a recommendation, *but be sure to insist that the recommended teacher bases his or her technique on classical ballet.* Then do the following:

— watch a class; examine the students carefully (they

should not have bulky muscles such as one gets from aerobic training; the muscles should be long and lean).

— find out the teacher's *technique;* how much of the class is based on this technique, and, in the case of modern dance, how much of the class is based on improvization (too much emphasis on improvization means that base technique will be undeveloped).

Many dancers have their first introduction to modern dance in college. It is here, as Ruth Ambrose of the Boston Conservatory says, "the dancer has a chance to say something and coming to a college gives the opportunity to spend four years in a nice confined place to develop technique and ideas." Modern dance doesn't demand a certain type of body the way ballet does. There is no such thing as the "perfect" modern dance body. Yet, stringent standards still need to be observed. The fact is that overweight, wide hips, tight joints and unstretched feet remain unacceptable, no matter the dance form — whether it's ballet or modern dancing. "Most of our companies do have ballet training side by side with modern training," says Ruth Ambrose, and because of that the ballet body remains the general standard by which the modern dance body will be judged.

The same holds true for jazz dancing, though, once again there is no such thing as the "perfect" jazz dance body. "The thicker-built dancer has more of a chance here," says Rochelle McReynolds, "though they still have to take their ballet classes, too. When I look at a ballet dancer, I examine the extension of the line; when I look at a jazz dancer, I examine the same thing, but I'm more accepting. I search for texture rather than position. I try to find texture from beginning to end."

And texture, of course, is not quite so limiting.

But ballet remains the basis.

When I was seventeen, I enrolled at the Arts Educational Schools in London to continue my high school and dance training. After years of ballet training, I was upset to find we were required to take classes in all forms of dance, including tap. Such a come-down!

121

I did everything to avoid these classes but without success, and I reluctantly learned what was offered. It was not with great joy, however. At the end of my first year I signed up for an audition with Emile Littler Productions. They were presenting a musical Christmas show, and I was curious about the repertoire. To my surprise I discovered that the additional dance forms I had learned gave me an edge over the other dancers who had had straight ballet training only.

Yes, I got the job, and the lesson stayed with me. For years, whenever I was on lay-off, I was always able to get a nightclub or musical theatre job to tide me over.

Part VI:
Summer Programs

The committed teenager dances everywhere.

"I really enjoyed the summer! I feel I accomplished a lot."

"This place is wonderful."

"It was a growing experience for me."

"... a most beautiful dance experience filled with love and understanding."

"I really love [this summer program]..."

Reactions to one summer dance program from one group of dancers and teachers. They mirror the feelings of countless others in summer dance programs from one end of the country to the other. The truth is that, by and large, students and teachers have a good time in a well-managed summer dance program. Things are more flexible. There is less pressure, and new friends are made. Frequently, too, the program is located in a retreat-like setting far from crowds, noise and city temptations.

And they actually learn, too. According to Francia Russell, director of Seattle's Pacific Northwest Ballet which has its own summer program, the students "get exposure to the ballet idiom, to jazz, modern dance, character dancing and musical appreciation. We want them to be productive."

The summer dance program world is not large, and those

who have experienced it find the occasional surprise. Take Lisa who is currently dancing with a medium-sized international company. Recently, she and the company were in Italy, performing and touring for an extended period. "One day," Lisa says, "I was rehearsing, and I looked up to see a young woman in conversation with the ballet mistress. I thought she looked familiar, but from the distance I wasn't sure. She was pointing at me, and the ballet mistress was nodding. All of a sudden it hit me! Joelle! My roommate at the summer ballet program I attended as a young teenager. 'Joelle?' I mouthed. 'Lisa?' she laughed. It had been six years since we had seen one another. After rehearsal we talked and found out each of us was with a ballet company, and both of us were touring Italy! And neither of us knew the other was around."

The summer ballet program should be approached a step at a time. First, ask the young dancer's teacher about the various programs. Get an idea of which ones seem more suitable, more agreeable. But note this... if the teacher tries to downplay the importance of the summer dance experience, and urges instead that the young dancer stay in her studio for the summer, warning bells should ring. The teacher's interests may be more her own economic loss than anything to do with her student's dance future. Teachers who don't encourage students to have a broadening experience, such as a summer dance program, may be unsure of their own teaching abilities.

And this will ultimately reflect on the quality of the teaching the young dancer will get.

But let's assume the summer dance experience is encouraged and promoted. What then?

— make a list of questions concerning living conditions, training, food, locale, supervision, travel and recreation opportunities.

— the young dancer should talk with others who have attended summer programs, even talk with parents of those who have attended summer programs.

— call the director of the program and ask for names of parents of former students that live nearby. Be ready to ask these parents for some answers.

There are, in effect, four basic items a young dancer should consider with a summer program:

1. Are there performing opportunities?

2. Is the setting rural or urban?

3. Is there a company affiliation?

4. Who are the master teachers?

In Burklyn Ballet Theatre, for example, they provide major performing opportunities at least once a week with a one and one-half hour program, fully costumed and produced on a professional stage. Directors, like Bruce Marks of the Boston Ballet, find the performing aspects of the program most valuable. "Burklyn is doing it the right way," he says. "They are teaching the students their craft, instead of simply teaching them how to take a class."

But it is not the only way. Other programs do not offer major performance opportunities, preferring, instead, to concentrate on technique and instruction. The choice is an individual one.

The question of where the program is located can be important. Marcia Dale Weary, director of the Central Pennsylvania Youth Ballet, recommends her students attend a summer program away from their usual environment. "As they get older," she says, "I think it's good for them. They see what it's really like to be in a summer school. They don't have regular school, so they don't have anything else to worry about, and they can concentrate on ballet." A rural or urban school is really a matter of individual choice. The Pennsylvania Ballet keeps its summer program going in downtown Philadelphia, while the Atlanta Ballet boards its students at nearby Oglethorpe University which can be reached from downtown by public transportation. On the other hand, Ballet West in Salt Lake City, Utah, moves to lovely Aspen, Colorado, for the summer, and of course, Burklyn Ballet Theatre operates on a quiet college campus in rural Vermont. What is most appealing to the young dancer is really the key, and for some the summer program setting is crucial.

The company affiliation aspect of a summer program can be the most important consideration, especially if the young dancer is determined to join a specific company. Francia Russell, director of Pacific Northwest Ballet Company, puts it succinctly. "If the dancer has decided that a certain company is where she wants to work eventually, then stick with it." Join the company's summer program. Go back year after year.

Many major companies do have summer programs. The Boston Ballet, for instance, has two summer programs, one for those fourteen and over (which operates out of the ballet company studios), and the other for younger dancers (which goes into residency at a nearby college campus). According to Bruce Wells, assistant director of the Boston Ballet, "The value of a summer program is to allow the child exposure to many different aspects of the dance medium. It's much more intensive, accelerated movement, and it puts the children into the position of deciding if they really want to become dancers."

In New York the School of American Ballet also has a summer program, and of course, this could be one way for a young dancer to discover whether she or he might eventually seek a place with the New York City Ballet. Regular, full-time students at SAB, on the other hand, are sometimes encouraged to look elsewhere during the summer. "Try a summer program in some other area of the country," SAB director, Robert Lindgren, says he tells students from time to time. "Aspire to the New York City Ballet. That's fine. But like a lot of things in life, once something can't be attained, you have to change and get your priorities in order and say 'my goals have now changed, too'."

The non-company affiliated programs may not bring the young dancer into daily contact with particular company personnel, but that shouldn't create any less opportunity. At Burklyn Ballet Theatre, for example, the master teachers have come from ballet companies across the country, and they are always looking for talented young dancers. Robert Barnett, artistic director of the Atlanta Ballet, and who has taught at Burklyn, says that except for an audition in New York and one in Atlanta, "I look for company dancers while I guest teach in summer programs."

The point of it all is this: company affiliated or non-affiliated, a summer program provides a young dancer with exposure to professional ballet teaching which may — note, *may* — lead to further opportunity.

We should be aware of one thing, however: there is an age consideration in whether a young dancer should attend a summer program. Most responsible directors don't take children under twelve years old because the training is intense (as much as three to five classes per day, and in some cases, five or six days per week), and the young child would tend to get overtired. At

Burklyn we accept dancers younger than twelve—occasionally—if they show unusual talent and have a teacher's recommendation. Even then we insist on a parent interview, and we gauge our acceptance on whether an older brother or sister, or some other dancer from the same studio, is coming, too. The parent is informed that acceptance is conditional, that if the child is not happy or does not seem to fit in, she/he will be sent home without a refund of fees. What this does is to make sure that parents and children understand the fragility of the decision and that acceptance into the program is only under the most unusual circumstances.

> *As a child, I was sent to a boarding program at the age of six that had no dance program. I was miserable and cried nightly. Six years later—at the age of twelve—I was given the chance to attend one of the finest boarding dance programs in Great Britain. My fear of being away from my family, based on the earlier experience, caused me to refuse the new chance. Had I accepted, I would have studied with two of the finest ballet teachers ever to emigrate from Russia, the Legat brothers. No doubt my career would have benefited greatly from the training, and to this day I have great regrets about what I did.*

For the child under twelve, the best approach is to search out a "camp" which may have some form of dance expression associated with it. There are a number of directories available in the local library which will describe these offerings, and of course, there is always the school guidance counselor. Look, too, in the Sunday New York Times Magazine. There is a camp directory that is kept current in almost every weekly issue. While these programs do teach minimal classical ballet, they also offer arts and crafts and other recreation, and some go far enough to provide an introduction to dance and theatre arts. For the budding young dancer it is a way to continue an interest in dance, while not being pressured to learn ballet movement that would be beyond his/her physical capabilities.

But once twelve years of age is reached, the summer dance experience awaits!

Auditioning is where it begins. For Bruce Wells of the Boston Ballet, it means a multi-city tour, searching for young people for the two summer programs. "I audition two hours for

131

each program," he says, "and I require all those auditioning to take a complete class. What I'm looking for is actual ballet technique and talent, and at the end of it I offer a place in our summer program only to some people." He looks for two specific things in these summer program auditions: "No overweight and good proportion. I want to see a nice flow of movement."

All directors look for particular things during these auditions. Francia Russell of Pacific Northwest Ballet, looks for the dancer or dancers that might eventually fit her company; ones with long, slender legs, high extension and "a good attitude." Robert Barnett, of the Atlanta Ballet, won't take anyone under five-foot-three or over five-foot-seven because he knows they will never fit in his company, and he uses the summer program to seek apprentices for his company.

From January through March, the major summer programs audition dancers for acceptance and scholarships. See the January issue of "Dance Magazine" each year. There are multitudes of display ads that list summer programs and it is here that initial summer program choices should be made. Note, too, that in May, "Dance Magazine" also offers a summer program pull-out section, repeating much of the January information, (by this time many of the summer programs are full). The scholarships range from complete tuition to minimal stipends which will, at least, reinforce the young dancer's self-esteem. Auditions for summer programs with San Francisco Ballet, School of American Ballet, Boston Ballet, Burklyn Ballet Theatre, Pacific Northwest Ballet and most others are given throughout the country. Although auditions are not mandatory for acceptance in many of the programs, it does give the director a chance to see each young dancer, and possibly award scholarship funds.

Of all the auditions, the ones at SAB are the most crowded because many full-tuition scholarships are available. For the parent, the important thing to know is that since SAB is in New York City, the uncertain questions of housing and general supervision during the summer program must be understood. Contrast this with the prestige of the SAB program, and the parental dilemma is obvious.

At Burklyn Ballet Theatre, we use auditions to search for young dancers with a true love of the art, a natural talent and musicality, a body that has potential, technique, an attitude that will benefit from the master teacher's demands for growth — a dancer who loves to perform.

The benefits of a summer program are obvious:

— new and different teachers and directors.

— new and different styles and syllabuses.

— new and different locations and experiences.

— new and different choreography.

Add to all of this the chance for exciting interaction with new friends from other parts of the country, the social benefits of the summer program. "For the children from out of town, just meeting other children who are doing the same thing can be pretty great!" says Marcia Dale Weary, director of the Central Pennsylvania Youth Ballet. "The children in my school are like a family. They visit each other almost as cousins, and their friendships last forever — sometimes they are forty years old and they *still* have those same friends."

Dancers are with a group where everyone understands their love and dedication. They all empathize with the desire to dance ten hours a day and perform every week. Students and di-

Summer programs add a chance for exciting interaction with new friends.

rectors form a bond that lasts and lasts . . .

"We get regular phone calls and letters from former students seeking career advice."

"We hear continually about former students' marriages, children and unbreakable friendships with other former students."

"We see former students for social engagements whenever we audition in their cities or towns."

Part VII:

The Later Years
(ages 16-18)

Many colleges offer professionally oriented dance programs.

—————Chapter 1:—————
College Dance
Alternative

Skidmore College, Bennington College, Virginia Intermont College, Brigham Young University, Louisville University, Texas Christian University, Oberlin College, University of California at Irvine... a few of the many colleges and universities that have regular, professionally-oriented dance programs.

Is it one path to a dance career?

Listen to a response from New York's Juilliard School where the dance division prepares its students for performing dance careers: "Students work with a wide variety of choreographers and company directors during their stay. Recent graduates have gone into Joffrey Ballet, Martha Graham Dance Co., Jose Limon Dance Co., Merce Cunningham Dance Co., Hartford Ballet, Alvin Ailey Dance Co...."

With more than one-hundred college and university dance programs available, a dancer seeking higher education need not assume that the separate alternatives are mutually exclusive. One *can* go to college and still pursue a dance career!

— "The University Department of Ballet has been close-ly affiliated with Ballet West since its inception... the

Ballet West roster includes several former University graduates . . ." *(University of Utah)*

— "Extensive performance and student choreography opportunities in formal and informal concerts, lecture demonstrations and touring . . ." *(Kansas State University)*

— "Ours is a university dance training program for students interested in performance careers . . ." *(Southern Methodist University)*

Those that attend a college or university with a dance career still in mind have already put aside the incessant urge to give up everything *now*! To wrap themselves in a career *now*! They have made a choice that academics should not be dropped merely because they have reached seventeen or eighteen years of age. The thirst for knowledge lingers in them, and in many instances, it is knowledge specifically related to dance. Dance majors in college, for example, can expect to take courses in ballet, modern and jazz techniques, anatomy, kinesiology, choreography, music and teaching technique, notation, production skills and arts administration. These are in addition to other academic courses in the humanities and/or the sciences, but the result is to enlarge the student's perspectives and to open up other avenues of experiences. "College gives the dancer the opportunity to spend four years in a nice, confined place," says Ruth Ambrose, Dean of Dance at the Boston Conservatory. She sees this as a positive happening because it allows the dancer "to develop technique and ideas," in a supportive atmosphere and with others who are similarly motivated.

For the ballet dancer, however, the choice cuts both ways because dancers "know long before college age they want ballet, and so they tend to leave school." Ballet companies are always seeking young people, and this adds pressure on the young ballet dancer to try a professional career without college. Ruth Ambrose admits, "We have had people here who have gone on to fine ballet careers, but it is more the modern dancer who will stick it out and benefit from the college experience."

But if the ballet dancer insists on college, there are pleasant benefits. College dance programs are often the first chance a classical ballet student will get to study modern dance in depth. Many fine, modern dancers in professional companies are those who have studied classical ballet for years before attending college. Then, once they get exposed to the personal approach that modern dance offers so effectively, they find themselves fitting their own style and training to the art form.

The result can be a dynamic new career path, carrying a special blend of individualism and personal satisfaction:

> *Floyd had taken several years of ballet training before he entered college, but in his sophomore year he became aware that modern dance classes were being offered at a nearby studio by a teacher with a good local reputation. He signed up and found himself enjoying the experience.*
>
> *At the same time he was chosen to dance in a performance of the regional ballet company connected with his college, and midway through the year he auditioned for me and was accepted at Burklyn Ballet Theatre.*
>
> *While at Burklyn, he had classes and some choreography training in the Martha Graham technique. He asked me if he could have extra class time because he found this experience so enjoyable. Both the teacher and I agreed readily, and he did so well that at the end of the summer the teacher called the Graham School in New York and arranged for him to have two weeks in their training program. He fully intended to return to college and continue with his dance training.*
>
> *But after seeing him, the Graham School invited him to return on scholarship for a two-week Christmas dance seminar. Throughout the fall he continued with his ballet and modern classes at college, and then he came back to New York to the Graham seminar.*
>
> *By the end of the first week, he was invited to join the company where he has continued to dance to this day . . .*

Choreography also is one of the areas that college or university training can offer. For the dancer who wants to choreograph, performing vehicles are essential. Ruth Ambrose puts it in perspective: "In college it's very nice because you have the dancers in the department, you have the studios to rehearse in, and you can create as much as you can do. Whereas, if you try to do these things independently you have to rent the studio, find the dancers, and it gets very difficult and expensive."

There are classes in choreography in most college and university dance programs, and careers in choreography are encouraged. The percentages of students continuing with choreography vary with the institution, but most can point to some participation at least. In a recent survey we asked the question: "What percentage of your students continue choreography?" Among the answers were the following:

— 25% — UCLA

— 75% — University of New Mexico

— 25% — University of Maryland

— 10% — College of St. Theresa

For these institutions, and for many others, training and practice in choreography is not a simple end in itself. It can be, and often is, a means to an ultimate career that is the product of exposure to the discipline while on campus.

There is always the teaching alternative, of course. A dance career includes a dance *teaching* career, and to acquire these skills as well as unchallenged acceptability among educators, a Bachelor of Fine Arts, or even a Master of Fine Arts, degree is necessary. Colleges and universities provide this training and offer a sufficiently rounded curriculum so that academic and dance training are interrelated. The degree, in and of itself, doesn't make a dancer more acceptable to company artistic directors, nor does it guarantee that one's level of ballet will be any more dramatic, fulfilling or expressive. What it does guarantee, however, is that one's knowledge of the ballet art form — its history, its variations, its creation — is sufficiently high so that others can be taught to appreciate the same things.

Suppose, now, the decision to attend college has been made, and the major remaining question is *what* college. Some dance programs are simply inappropriate for certain people, and there are ways to winnow down the list so a reasonable fit can be attained. First, however, get a copy of *Dance Magazine's* "College Dance Guide," published annually. Here will be a brief description of every college or university program along with some information about curriculum and entrance requirements. Discuss it with school guidance counselors, and once a list of acceptable schools has been made visit the campus and do the following:

— ask to participate in, or observe, several dance classes.

— ask whether the school requires auditions for acceptance or for placement.

— ask whether the dance department is part of a fine and performing arts department or imbedded in the physical education department (the former is much better).

— seek out and examine the theatre and performing spaces on campus.

— ask whether the dance department attends any of the regional or national College Dance Festivals.

— discover whether the dance *teaching* majors have an opportunity to teach in local studios or in schools.

— find out where, and to whom, choreographic students show their work.

— seek out some of the dance majors, find out about their previous training (recital schools or regional ballet companies).

Intensity of interest, commitment to student progress, fine tuning of ultimate dance career aspirations — all of these things vary with individual colleges or universities. But there is no doubt that a large dance performing, dance choreographing, dance teaching field of opportunity exists for the young ballet dancer who has decided that a full-time dance career *now!* isn't what she/he wants. Can't it be just as exciting, just as rewarding to hear from a dance department administrator such as Barbara Hamblin of the University of Utah, Department of Ballet, who writes:

"We are very proud of our department, its history and traditions, and the fact that it is not within a modern department but a separate entity. We are very excited about our new dance facility which will be one of only three in the nation built specifically for dance. Construction is on schedule ..."

As an apprentice, dancers hone their performing skills.

------Chapter 2:------
A Full Time Dance
Career Now?

The last two years of high school, young dancers on the down slope of secondary education, seventeen- and eighteen-year-olds on the verge of adulthood.

One more major dance decision to make. Teens huddling with parents on an ages-old dilemma:

Am I a dancer, or what?

Do I want a college education?

Maybe I *need* a college education.

Maybe not.

The scene can be replayed over and over, every year, in homes across the country.

"I'll be too old to dance professionally if I go to college."

"Your father and I loved our college years."

"You weren't dancers."

"It's time to get serious about your life."

"I *am* serious..."

Make no mistake, the seventeen- or eighteen-year-old dancer can be wholly dedicated to art and dance prospects. After eight to ten years of class several times a week, and a continuing year-round dosage of ballet, the young dancer is not undergoing some fanciful whim when she/he ponders the merits of pursuing a professional ballet career at the expense of a beckoning college education.

Take Becky Metzger, for example. At age fifteen, she came to New York after being accepted by the School of American Ballet. She continued her academic education at New York's Professional Children's School, and then when she became eighteen, she had the hard choice to face. The choice wasn't made easier when the New York City Ballet offered her an apprenticeship contract. Some would have chucked any further schooling to devote themselves totally to ballet. Not Becky. Instead, she applied to, and was accepted by, Barnard College, while simultaneously agreeing to the apprenticeship contract with the New York City Ballet. For the moment, anyway, she could pursue both options.

Not for long, however. Just a few months later, she was offered a company contract by the New York City Ballet. The dilemma presented itself anew, but this time she chose differently. "I told Barnard I wouldn't be coming," she says. "I feel I should put all my energies into my dancing right now. I'll go to college one day, but not for a while."

It is only proper that a parent should be concerned about a young dancer's continuing education. The ballet art form is not only demanding physically, but its opportunities are limited, except for the exceedingly talented, the overly lucky, or some combination of the two. A young dancer with reasonable ballet credentials might find herself/himself mired in an unrewarding ballet career and without the educational resources to change directions. It is not a picture that can calm parental uncertainty.

"At least get that college degree behind you!"

"Great. I graduate, and no one wants me. Too old, they'll say..."

Ballet does demand youth. During the early months in a company, a dancer hones the skills learned through the years and years of training. The physical demands are rigorous, frequent twelve-hour days, for example, while rehearsing for performances, plus daily ballet classes that run sometimes two-three hours each. When on tour, there is never enough time to sleep, eat, rehearse, do laundry, set hair or seek general relaxation. Performances come at a dizzying speed, and transportation from performance site to performance site can often be at the most inconvenient times and in the most uncomfortable manner.

My two children approached the college versus company dilemma in different ways, yet both serve to illustrate how ballet decisions must be made at a young age:

At eighteen, my son was undecided about his career. He had spent years backstage with me, learning the intricacies of technical direction. Should he go with a ballet company or start college? He finally decided to enter college with a major in theatre technical direction. The combination didn't work, and he changed to a full business major. Now he has his business degree and a skill beyond the limits of ballet technical direction. What's he doing with it? He's back with ballet — his first love — as a technical director. BUT he knows he could move into another career without difficulty.

My daughter is a dancer, and at age seventeen, she rejected any thought of college. She was offered an apprenticeship contract with a major ballet company, and for her the career path was clear and uncomplicated. Two years later she joined another major ballet company, this time as a company member, but she sensed she needed something more in her life. So she started evening classes at a local community college. Nothing overly complicated, nothing too time consuming. But a start. "I know that eventually I will get a college degree," she tells me. "But right now I'm at the best age for ballet, so that has to come first."

Age alone, does not necessarily tell a seventeen- or eighteen-year-old that a ballet career may be lost forever if not adopted by a certain time. For some teenagers the years of training coupled with the limited opportunities may put the idea of a ballet career into a receding future, even though they have talent and desire. Impatience plays a part in this, as does constant comparison with peers — do I *really* have it? . . . so-and-so was in a company by sixteen . . . my extension is *never* high enough . . . that's the twelfth straight audition I've failed in . . . my teachers have never believed in me . . .

At the moment of the career dilemma, self-doubt flows through the young dancer's mind, unchecked and unappeased. The college alternative is certainly appropriate, but it should be chosen because the young dancer sees it as the next step on an affirmative career path and because of uncertainty that professional ballet will accept her unconditionally. Only with absolute certainty should the non-ballet alternative be followed. Anything less than that certainty could sidetrack an ultimate ballet career.

Marcia Dale Weary, artistic director of the Central Pennsylvania Youth Ballet, tells a story that highlights how important it is to understand the clay that will mold the professional ballet dancer. "I had a little girl in my school that no one ever thought had talent. Her shoulders were too high, her extension was bad, her feet were poor. Person after person would ask, 'Why do you encourage her?' But this little girl loved ballet, and I could feel the desire in her. Nothing I could say or do would convince her to try something else. One day she came to class in a leg cast and insisted on trying to keep up, including doing grand battements. So I started working with her, and gradually she got her extension up, she worked and worked on her turnout, she learned to hold her arms down so they had a better line to her shoulder, and she developed her feet so they were adequate, at least. Such desire!" Now, years later, it has paid off. "She's a lead dancer with a major state ballet company," Marcia Dale Weary says with a smile.

The career choice, then, is the product of many things, and talent may not be the most significant. Desire and determination play an important part, and the choice must be weighed with this in mind.

Suppose, therefore, the young dancer at age seventeen or eighteen has decided on a ballet career *now!*

— get the *Dance Magazine Annual.* Make a list of all the ballet companies. Write to them and ask for a summary of their repertory and a copy of a recent program — *be sure to include a large, stamped, self-addressed envelope.*

— read the dancer's biographies in the program. It will show where and what type of training the director seems to choose, how long dancers have been in the company (this will give a clue to amount of turnover and relative company morale).

— check the photos in the program. How well does the corps de ballet work? Are they all synchronized in the white ballets? Is "line", "jumping", "pas de deux", classical or contemporary repertoire what the director looks for?

— check the list of contributors on the program. Is the company well funded? Are the majority of contributors corporate or personal? (Corporate contributors give a company more stability and longevity.)

— write to the Chamber of Commerce in the cities where the companies are located. Ask for literature and some feeling about citizen reaction to having a ballet company there. Is the city proud to have a ballet company? Does it have broad support?

Career or no career, college or no college, the dilemma faces parents and young dancers alike. A career in ballet remains a fragile choice throughout the young dancer's training years. There are always other alternatives. A commitment to dance, however, carries with it the focus of energies that can mold a young person into a positive, mature adult providing a joy to many others. For parents the choice may not be between a career in ballet and a college education, as between a young person's self-fulfillment and surrender to self-doubt. In the end there has to be ultimate faith in the young dancer's vision of herself/himself. No better is it illustrated than by an apprentice dancer with the Atlanta Ballet who says:

"My parents are helping me with living expenses, and they consider that to be money that would have paid for my room and board in college. I guess when, and if, I get around to going to college, I'll have to pay for it myself, but right now all I want to do is dance."

A performance photograph can be used to accompany your resumé.

AFTERWORD
What Next?

"Angela! Telephone."

It was my daughter calling from the performing arts school where she was about to graduate, seventeen now, and dedicated to ballet. "Mom . . . where do I find out about auditions? What do I need to do? How should I prepare?"

Silence. Nothing flowed to my mind. All I had was a blank. We'd been so intent on training her through the school years, we'd simply assumed the career steps would take care of themselves.

"Mom?"

Somewhere, I knew I could provide her answers. I had to think, to do some calling around, maybe even a little reading.

"Mom!"

Ballet was my life. I ran a successful company and a successful school. If I couldn't supply these answers, who could? What about parents who *don't* have a ballet background?

"Let me call you back in a day or two," I said, appalled by the notion that I couldn't put my finger on such information without further thought. If a young dancer at the threshold of a career needs answers like these, I thought, why couldn't I supply them?

Unless... there wasn't anything readily available.

Sure, books and articles were out there, but the more I researched, the more convinced I became that nothing existed which could provide answers to the many questions a young, professional dancer would have as she or he moved across the threshold of a career. My daughter, in fact, became my guinea pig, and as she began her professional ballet life, first as an apprentice in a major company, then as a full company member in another well-known company, then, finally, as a soloist, her questions, her concerns, formed a chain of subjects that would stretch from her pre-career training to the heart of her professional life. In effect, my daughter provided me a thoroughly rounded look at what a young professional ballet dancer wants to know.

Suddenly I saw things more clearly. *The Parents Book of Ballet* was being written for parents with less knowledge than I had about ballet. It was about things that parents had repeatedly asked me through the years — schools, teachers, training, technique. Now a strange thing was happening... I was starting to address dancers, as well as their parents. I was pointing comments towards the professionals themselves.

Could there be a new book in all this?

A short time after the first telephone call, came another. "Mom, where do I get photographs?"

She meant professional photographs, of course. Before I could respond, she asked, "How do I do a resumé?"

Then, "Are professional auditions like those I've done for summer programs? How do I find them?..."

My mind worked furiously, even as I tried to respond. Auditions, photos, resumés, summer programs... "Let's take things one step at a time," I suggested.

"I *need* to know!" she said.

So do a lot of other young dancers, I thought.

I started keeping notes of her questions. When she was about to join her first company as an apprentice, she called. "What's it going to be like on the first day? Where do I stand at the barre?" As the months progressed, she learned about the company structure and why it was important to attend receptions and parties with other company members and company sponsors.

A year later she faced the uncertainty of contract renewal. "If they keep me as an apprentice for another year, what should I do? Can I ask the director for a recommendation if I want to leave? Will he help me and call other directors? Should I use the

PAMELA E. WHITEHILL

A good composite resumé photograph is of great importance before auditioning for a professional company.

same photos if I look for another job?"

"What do *you* think?" I said, parrying for time.

"I'm not sure."

Six weeks later she was proudly carrying a contract as a full-time member of a foreign company. No more apprenticeships to serve. But the questions still came. "Is my contract like the contracts in other companies? How does my salary compare? Should I join the union?"

More notes for my file, more research to do. "I think you

have a lovely job," I told her, "and I think I can answer most of your questions."

"It sure helps, Mom."

During the following year, the company toured throughout Europe, Canada and the United States, traveling by bus and plane. A Monday here, a Tuesday there... packing, unpacking, never catching up on sleep. The questions continued to come: "What should I pack for Italy? We're going to be in three different climates the next two weeks. How can I wear the same thing? The artistic director thinks I should gain five pounds. What should I do? The administrative staff doesn't speak English. Should I take special lessons so I can communicate with them?"

Company life, and the young professional's daily struggle. "I think you should decide what is in your best interests and in the best interests of your career. You are a professional ballet dancer now, and that means you are an adult. Other dancers have the same questions you do. What do they say?"

"Why isn't there a book that gives us the answers?"

I thumbed through my notes over the past two years.

Questions, questions... about auditioning, choreographing, apprenticeships, backstage etiquette, company relationships, unions, injuries, lay-offs, touring, casting, joining a foreign company... it could make a book.

"How does *A Professional Ballet Career — Now!* sound?"

"You're serious, aren't you?"

"Sure am."

APPENDIX

*Samples of customary
ballet school forms,
Regional Ballet standards,
regulations and
Nutcracker information
for parents*

(sample)

Burklyn Ballet Theatre
Photo Release Form

I (we), the undersigned, hereby waive and release any and all rights we may have regarding ownership or use of photographs bearing my (our) image taken while at Burklyn, and grant permission to said Burklyn Ballet Theatre to use and display said photographs for commercial or non-commercial use.

Date: _____ /s/ _____

/s/ _____

_____

I hereby certify that I am the parent or guardian of _____ and I do hereby give my consent under the terms above.

_____

Signature of Parent or Guardian

_____

Signature of Witness

(sample)

Dayton Contemporary Dance Company II Standards*

I. All Dancers:

1. Must attend all required classes and rehearsals at our studios.

2. Must be on time and properly attired for all classes, rehearsals and performances.

3. Students will not be allowed in class after it has begun without the permission of the teacher. Counted as an absence.

4. Will be fined for absenteeism from rehearsal. (Each dancer is allowed only three excused absenses during the commitment term, September through June. All other absences are inexcused.)

5. Will not be allowed in class or rehearsal inappropriately attired. Counted as an absence.

6. Must maintain an adequate grade average in school as required by parents' standards, so that he or she can meet the demands required by the company.

7. Must maintain weight required by the company director.

8. Will perform when the Artistic Director feels that the dancer is able to perform.

9. Must make full season commitment.

10. Professionalism from each dancer is expected at all times in all circumstances. The director, teacher or guest choreographer will accept nothing less and has the authority to dismiss any dancer from class or rehearsal not working at a professional level. Counted as an absence.

We want our company to excel on all levels, technically and professionally. You can help by following the Standards accordingly.

II. Performance, Dress Rehearsals and Stage Etiquette:

1. No excuses allowed for tardiness or absence.

2. Dancers must perform from offstage wall to offstage wall for entrances and exits.

3. All crossovers, entrances and exits made discreetly without touching or disturbing cyc, curtain, scrim, wings or lights

4. Dancers will always be considerate of one another, extending due courtesy and respect to each other at all times.

5. Dancers must extend 150% at all times.

Proper Attire

Ladies:

1. Tights and leotard.

2. Must pull hair back into bun if over one-inch of growth. No bangs, baby hair, ponytails. All hair pulled off forehead, face and neck.

3. Must shave underarms and legs for all dress rehearsals and performances. Absolutely no crotch hair is visible.

4. Must have trimmed and unpainted fingernails.

5. Must wear dance girdles (for your protection).

6. Shoes when required.

7. No jewelry in class or rehearsal.

Men

1. Tights, leotard or neat T-shirt, belt.

2. Must be clean shaven.

3. Hair must be neatly cut off of forehead, face, ears and neck.

4. Must wear dance belts (for your protection).

5. No jewelry in class or rehearsal.

6. Shoes when required.

Leg warmers are used with permission of teacher. However, they must fit securely on the legs and not hide the form of the leg.

Absolutely no plastic pants, ankle warmers, bulky sweaters or loose T-shirts. This is not the cast of "Fame."

No sweatbands (forehead or wrists).

III. In General:

You must have your own dance gear at the beginning of the year and maintain it throughout. Jeraldyne's School of Dance is not a supply house for forgetful dancers.

Check bulletin board daily. Sign in when you arrive.

Evaluations will be held at end of Winter and Spring Concerts.

These Dayton Contemporary Dance Company II standards are published with permission of the Artistic Director, Jeraldyne Blunden.

(sample)

Boston Ballet Company
Nutcracker Performance

Dear Parents:

"Nutcracker" time is fast approaching. We have prepared this letter about backstage rules.

Once you're involved, you will wish you weren't and you'll swear that you won't let your kid(s) be in it next year. Don't worry, *everyone* says that — and most come back!

So you've decided to let him/her be in "Nutcracker" anyway. Rehearsals seem endless, casting is always changing, tickets will probably be sold out before you get the performance or price you want.

And now to business:

Dressers

We will provide professional dressers for the students. *All* costuming will be done by dressers. This will mean that students can get into their costumes themselves, but under no circumstances may they be hooked, pinned, or zippered by each other. Only the dressers will perform this task. This means that:

1. The students will have to dress at an appointed time, (perhaps earlier than before).

2. They will have to remain standing after they are dressed and be careful of costumes.

3. They must keep their personal clothing and belongings in one area, separate from the costumes, and

4. They must hang up all costume pieces after performing.

Children's Supervision

There will be no parent volunteers. In recent years we initiated this policy, and the backstage confusion was diminished considerably. The students will be supervised by a staff hired by the Boston Ballet Company for this purpose only. These staff members will:

1. Make sure that all the children have arrived and call for substitutes if necessary.

2. Escort students to stage door and wait with them until parents pick them up after performance. (This means that *no* parents will be allowed past the doorman at the stage door. Children may be paged to come to the stage door for messages, forgotten supplies, pickup, etc.)

3. Accompany each group to stage at appropriate time, and remain with them in wings and escort them back to dressing room.

Children's Duties

In addition to their performing, it will be the responsibility of each and every student to:

1. Keep their personal belongings together and separate from the costumes.

2. Arrive on time and adhere to schedules.

3. Bring quiet games and activities to remain occupied. There is much time spent waiting in the dressing rooms, and there will be no wandering or running in the corridors *at all*.

4. Provide supervisor with a note if viewing performances or any other irregularities in routine and,

5. Arrive with proper supplies and hair in place for performing.

Parents will *not be allowed into the house* (audience) *without a ticket. Parents are not allowed to wait backstage or downstairs. This will be enforced.*

The company will provide a Hospitality Room at the Park Plaza for the parents and family to wait in while their child/children perform. If your child is in Act One, you can pick him/her up at the stage door one hour after curtain time. If in the second act, they can be met one hour, 45 minutes after the curtain goes up. The children will be escorted to and supervised at the stage door until pickup.

Each cast will be in approximately twelve-eighteen performances each. Children will provide their own ballet slippers and performance tights in good condition, please. If shoes and tights are wearing out, please replace them. Please do not have your child arrive at the theatre with shoes that need to be taped, or with tights that have holes in them.

All parents will wait in the hospitality room or pick up their child/children at the stage door (on Stuart Street, opposite Jacob Wirth's).

We know that these rules sound very hard-nosed, but there are over seventy children in each "Nutcracker" performance, plus two parents each, brothers, sisters, grandparents, aunts, uncles, cats and dogs. Plus forty-five musicians, forty dancers, fifteen apprentices, stagehands and staff. The procedures listed above are standard to any professional ballet company and will make it safer and more pleasant for *all* involved.

Now for some good news:

The Company is providing the parents' Hospitality Room at the Park Plaza for family and parents to wait in while their child/children perform. To help parents defray the traveling expenses incurred in bringing their child/children to rehearsal and performances, the Company will pay each child $1.00 for each performance he/she is in. This reimbursement will be made at the end of February 1987.

Tickets

The ticket office at 553 Tremont St. will be open in early November from noon to 4 p.m. to accommodate parents. For *certain performances* we will limit ticket sales to four tickets per family for that performance. This is being done to give all families an equal chance to purchase good seats.

Please watch the board for date of parent ticket sales!

Please carefully consider all the aspects and commitments of having your child perform in "Nutcracker." It can be a rewarding "professional" theatre experience for you and your child.

Thank you,

THE BOSTON BALLET COMPANY

(sample)

Boston Ballet Company
Nutcracker
*Notes for Parents**

Hospitality Room

The Hospitality Room will once again be hosted by the Park Plaza Hotel, Park Square, open from 10 a.m. to 10 p.m. every performance day and dress rehearsal day, for parents and family waiting for child performers. The hospitality room will be the Back Bay Room (Room 401). Should the room be locked, please call security on any house phone.

There will be one phone in the hospitality room for incoming emergency calls only. Leave your number with your family or babysitter at home, but it must be for *emergency calls only.*

Outgoing calls must be made on the pay phones outside the room or in the lobby.

Restaurants in the hotel are as follows:

Cafe Rouge (moderately priced). Open seven days a week — Tuesday-Sunday, 7 a.m.-midnight; Monday, 7 a.m.-10 p.m.

Fox & Hound (jacket required), 11:30 a.m.-10:30 p.m.

There is a coffee pot and supplies in the hospitality room.

Blocking Rehearsals & Dress Rehearsal

Practice clothes for *Blocking Rehearsals.* Children should report to the theatre one-half hour prior to their rehearsal call. Blocking rehearsals are noted with the performance dates by part and cast.

There will be a make-up call for General Rehearsal. Children should report to the theatre for make-up at the time indicated on the make-up call sheet attached.

Parents of children rehearsing may attend the General Rehearsal *only.* However, it is a closed rehearsal and *not open* to the general public, and *only* parents of children participating are invited to attend. Everyone must enter via the main entrance on Tremont St., showing the student ID card of their child. They will be seated in the loge or balcony only, as the orchestra section is being made available by the Company to several special needs groups. Children performing in the Dress Rehearsal will enter through the stage door, as usual.

Parents are permitted to photograph from the loge during the General Rehearsal, providing no flash is used. However, the use of video cameras and/or recording devices is strictly forbidden in our contractual agreements with the Dancers', Musicians' and Stage Crew unions.

The front section of the orchestra is reserved for Boston Ballet Company photographers. Only photographers with a pass provided by the BBC marketing staff will be allowed in that section.

Admittance Backstage

No parents, family, or friends are permitted backstage before or during the show. All parents will please wait in the hospitality room or pick up their child/children at the stage door. After the performance is over, guests are welcome backstage. Your cooperation is appreciated.

Pick-Up

All Act I children will be escorted to the stage door at the conclusion of Act I, approximately one hour after the advertised curtain time.

All Act II children will be escorted to the stage door at the conclusion of Act II, approximately one hour and forty-five minutes after the advertised curtain time.

A supervisor will stay at the stage door until all children are picked up. Any children left will be brought back to the dressing room to wait.

Should you choose not to wait at the hospitality room, and you will be late in arriving at the stage door to pick up your child, please call the hospitality room and ask them to alert a children's supervisor when you come to the stage door to pick up your child/children.

Children Performing and Joining Parents in House

Only Act I Children will be permitted to join their parents who have tickets for a performance, *and only during intermission.* Any child who is to join his/her parents must be met by his/her parent and escorted to the seats. Children must be met at the entrance to backstage to your left as you are facing the stage (the door the chorus comes out of). If the child is too old to be "escorted he/she must show his/her ticket to the doorperson to enter the house during intermission. *No one* is allowed into the house with costume or make-up. *No one* is allowed into the house without a ticket.

Please make sure a children's supervisor is informed in writing if your child is to be met and escorted into the house during intermission to watch Act II.

Illness

Should your child be too ill to perform, please let us know as soon as possible so we may call a replacement:

Boston Ballet School, 9 a.m.-6 p.m., Monday-Saturday.
Boston Ballet Office and leave a message for Susan Ring.
The hospitality room, and have them contact children's supervisor, or Susan Ring, backstage.

Meals

Please be sure arrangements have been made for your child to eat between matinee and evening performances:

1. Either you or a family member pick them up and take them out;

2. Provide them with meal money and arrange for another parent to take your child out; or,

3. Pack a lunch.

Please make sure that the supervisor in charge of your child's group on a matinee/evening day are informed of your child's dinner arrangements. If you feel that your child is apt to forget to relay this message, please put it in writing.

A message basket will be located at the stage door for parents dropping off forgotten lunches, leotards, messages for child performers, etc.

Have children bring quiet games, books, homework, etc., to entertain themselves while waiting around backstage. We will be very firm with the children and assume that *they* will take responsibility for all of their free time. As part of a professional performance, we expect them to accept this challenge.

General Notes

Please check with the ballet company children's backstage supervisor or stage manager, regarding any questions.

Please be sure that your home phone number is correct on your child's registration card at the school. From these cards we will be obtaining all information necessary to contact performers for any reason.

Travel expense reimbursement checks ($1.00 per show) will be mailed to the children at the end of February.

No one will be allowed into the house unless they show their ticket for a seat to the doorperson.

No parents, family or friends are permitted backstage before or during the show. After the performance is over, guests are welcome backstage. After leaving the theatre, walk around to Stuart St. and enter through the stage door opposite Jacob Wirth's Restaurant.

Have a Happy Nutcracker, a Joyous Holiday, and thank you for your cooperation.

(sample)

Make-Up Calls

Nutcracker Children

Please arrive at the theatre fifteen minutes before make-up call.

Please report to the make-up room at the times indicated below, *on time, ready to be made up. No costumes.*

No costumes until one-half hour before you go on stage.

Noon curtain Make-up call	1:30 Dress	2:00 perf.	6:30 perf.	7:30 Sunday eve.
Party Clara Party	11:00 a.m.	12:30 p.m. Fritz Prologue	1:00 p.m.	5:30 p.m.	6:30 p.m.
Battle Bunny Soldier	11:15 a.m.	12:45 p.m. Mouse General	1:15 p.m.	5:45 p.m.	6:45 p.m.
Reindeer	11:15 a.m.	12:45 p.m.	1:15 p.m.	5:45 p.m.	6:45 p.m.
Act II Polichinelles Hoops	11:45 a.m.	1:15 p.m. Angels Dragonflies	1:45 p.m.	6:15 p.m.	7:15 p.m.

Shoe and Tights Requirements

Nutcracker Children

Party Children
  White knee socks or tights
  Black shoes with white elastic
  Two kilt boys — not white tights, black leotards, black
    elastics on shoes.

Bunny
  Brown shoes (Wardrobe will spray at dress rehearsal).

Baby Mouse
  Pink tights, pink shoes, leotard — any color.

Soldiers
　Black tights or knee socks, black shoes, black elastic.

Reindeer, Chinese Divertissement, Polichinelles
　White shoes, tights, leotard.

Angels, Dragonflies
　Ballet pink tights and pink shoes.

These Nutcracker Notes for Parents are published with permission of the Boston Ballet Co.

GLOSSARY

This glossary is not intended as a total compilation of classical ballet language. For this, one should seek out Gail Grant's *Dictionary of Classical Ballet,* Dover Publishing, New York. This glossary serves to explain the terms used in *The Parents Book of Ballet,* and some additional terms a young dancer might use at home.

Adagio: a series of poses, steps and movements performed to a slow musical tempo.

Academie de Dance: Dance School, refers to the first school of ballet started in France by Louis XIV in 1631.

Allegro: steps that are quick and lively performed to fast music.

Allongé: body extended, as in arabesque allongé.

Arabesque: a pose that shows the dancer's line. Arms are extended in front of the body, one leg lifted and extended behind the body.

Assemblé: a jump in which the legs are brought together in the air.

Attitude: a pose where the dancer stands on one leg, the other raised with a bent knee. Either in front, to the side or back.

Balancé: translates as "rocked". A step where the dancer shifts the weight from one side to the other.

Ballerina: a female, principal ballet dancer.

Ballet romantique: classical ballet as danced in the romantic period (usually telling a story).

Barre: a piece of wood or pipe attached to the wall. Dancers hold the barre to practice warm-ups.

Battement: a beating movement of the legs. There are many battement movements.

Batterie: a group of jumps where the legs beat multiple times in the air.

Bournonville, August: Danish dance choreographer and teacher, 1805-1879. Creator of the Danish Syllabus.

Bras: arms.

Bravura: spirited or bold execution of choreography.

Cecchetti Syllabus: a system of teaching ballet created by Enrico Cecchetti.

Character dance: folk dancing in classical style.

Chaînés: a series of small linked turns.

Changement de pied: jumps changing feet from back to front.

Choreography: the art of creating dances.

Corps de ballet: a group of dancers who form a background for the principal dancers.

Côté, de: to the side or sideways.

Cou-de pied: ankle.

Coupé: a petit allegro step.

Croisé: a direction of the body.

Dansuer: male dancer.

Degagé: a disengaged movement.

Demi: half.

Demi bras: arms halfway between bras bas and second position.

Demi pointes: half toe or on the ball of the foot.

Developé: an unfolding movement.

Directions of the body: position of the body in relation to the stage or room.

Ecarté: a direction of the body.

Echappé: an escaping movement.

Effacé: shaded, a position of the body.

Entrechat: a jump in which the dancer crosses and uncrosses the legs in the air many times.

En arriere: in a backwards direction.

En avant: traveling in a forwards direction.

En l'air: in the air, or off the ground.

En bas: low as in holding the arms low.

En face: a direction of the body, facing the audience.

Extension: the height of the leg to the front, side or back, as in extension to the arabesque.

Fouetté: a whipped movement, usually turning.

Grand: big, large or deep, usually refers to plié, battement, jeté, etc.

Jeté: a jump from one foot to the other, a thrown step.

Leotard: a tightfitting body suit.

Notation: a system of preserving choreography through writing or symbols.

Pas de bourée: a small traveling step.

Pas de chat: a jumping step.

Pas de deux: a dance for two people.

Passé: a passing movement, where the toe is raised and passed from front to back or back to front.

Piqué: a step or movement in which the body moves sharply.

Pirouette: a complete 360-degree turn of the body on one foot.

Plié: a bending movement of the knees.

Pointe: on the points or tips of the toes.

Port de Bras: movement of the arms with use of the head and body.

Relevé: to raise the body on to half, three-quarter, or full pointe.

Rond de Jambe; a round or circle movement of the leg.

Royal Academy of Dancing: a syllabus founded in Great Britain, based on the Danish, French and Italian methods.

Reverance: a curtsy or bow.

Sauté: jump.

Syllabus: a training system.

Turn out: the outward rotation of the legs and feet.

Tights: tightfitting stockings in solid colors used under a leotard.

Vaganova System: a syllabus created by Agrippina Vaganova (1879-1951) and used widely in Russia to train dancers for the Kirov and Bolshoi Ballet companies.

Variation: A solo dance, without corps de ballet participation.

BIBLIOGRAPHY

Ambrose, Kay. *Ballet Students Primer.* Alfred A. Knopf, Inc., New York, 1957.

Ambrose, Kay. *Beginners, Please!.* Adam & Charles Black, London, England, 1953.

Ambrose, Kay. *Ballet Lovers Companion.* Adam & Charles Black, London, England, 1949.

Cartwright, Hilary. *Dance As a Career.* Educational Explores, Reading, England, 1974.

Chujoy, Anatole. *Dance Encyclopedia.* Simon & Schuster, New York, 1968.

Cohen, Selma Jeanne. *Dance As a Theatre Art.* Harper & Row, New York, 1974.

Conyn, Cornelius. *Three Centuries of Ballet.* Australasian Publishing Co., Sydney, Australia, 1948.

de Mille, Agnes. *Dance to the Piper.* Little Brown & Co., Boston, Massachusetts, 1951.

de Mille, Agnes. *Speak to Me, Dance with Me.* Little, Brown and Co., Boston, Massachusetts, 1973.

Elkind, David. *The Hurried Child.* Wesley, 1981.

Geva, Tamara. *Split Seconds.* Harper & Row, New York, 1972.

Gordon, Suzanne. *Off Balance.* Pantheon Books, New York, 1972.

Horosko, Marian, Judith R. F. Kupersmith, M.D. *The Dancer's Survival Manual.* Harper & Row, New York, 1987.

Hurford, Daphne. *The Right Moves — A Dancer's Training.* Atlantic Monthly Press, New York, 1987.

Kirslemann, John, and Lavonne J. Dunne. *Nutrition Almanac.* McGraw Hill, 1975.

Kirsten, Lincoln, Stuart, Muriel & Dyer, Carlus. *The Classical Ballet.* Alfred A. Knopf, New York, 1973.

Kremetz, Jill. *A Very Young Dancer.* Alfred A. Knopf, Inc., New

York, 1976.

Lawson, Joan. *Teaching the Young Dancer.* Theatre Arts Books, New York, 1972.

Mara, Thalia, *1st, 2nd, 3rd and 4th Steps in Ballet,* Garden City Books, New York, 1956; reissued 1987 by Dance Horizons/ Princeton Book Company, Publishers.

Mara, Thalia, *The Language of Ballet: A Dictionary.* 1966; reissued 1987 by Dance Horizons/Princeton Book Company, Publishers.

Nielson, Eric Brandt. *Dance Auditions.* Princeton Book Company, Publishers, New Jersey, 1984.

Sammarco, M.D., G. James. *Sports Medicine.* W. B. Saunder Co., Philadelphia, Pennsylvania, 1983.

Terry, Walter. *On Pointe.* Dodd, Mead & Co., New York, 1963.

Vaganova, Agrippina. *Basic Principals of Classical Ballet.* Dover Publications, Inc., New York, 1969.

Vincent, L. M. *Competing with the Sylph.* 2nd. ed. Dance Horizons/ Princeton Book Company, Publishers, New Jersey, 1989.

Vincent, L. M. *The Dancer's Book of Health.* 1978; reissued 1988 by Dance Horizons/Princeton Book Company, Publishers.

About the Authors

WILLIAM P. NOBLE

With nine books to his credit (six co-authored with his late wife, June Noble), Bill Noble has been writing on a full-time basis since 1969. One of his books, *How to Live with Other People's Children* (Hawthorn, 1978), was a Book-of-the-Month Club Alternate, and a later work, *The Psychiatric Fix* (Delacorte, 1981), was a highly-lauded critique of the psychiatric profession. His latest book, *Shut Up! He Explained* (Paul S. Eriksson, 1987), is a Main Selection of the Writer's Digest Book Club, as was an earlier book, *Steal This Plot* (Paul S. Eriksson, 1985). He has been a Contributing Editor to *Window of Vermont Magazine,* and he has written numerous articles and short fiction for other periodicals such as *Yankee, Alfred Hitchcock's Mystery Magazine, Mike Shayne's Mystery Magazine, Adirondack Life, Dance Magazine, Pennsylvania Magazine, New England Guide, Atlantic City Press, Burlington Free Press, The Compass, National Fisherman, Nugget, Gent, Sir!*

He has appeared on more than sixty television and radio programs in connection with his writing, including *Today!, The David Suskind Show* and *Straight Talk.*

ANGELA WHITEHILL

As an artist committed to dance, Angela Whitehill has virtually done it all. Beginning as a professional dancer in the fifties with Emile Littler and Jack Hylton Productions in England, and the corps de ballet of Ballet de Paris, France, Angela moved on to become a ballet mistress and artistic director in the United States.

Over the years she won eight awards for her work in ballet instruction. For the past twelve years, serving as the artistic director of the Burklyn Ballet Theatre in Vermont, she has worked closely with the parents of students to guide young dancers on a career path to professional ballet. As evidence of her successful leadership, she has guided her own daughter through training and the audition process to a dancer's position with the Ballet de Montreal.

These many years of practical experience make her uniquely qualified to be the principal author of this book.

PHOTO CREDITS

Cover (top photo):
Lauren E. Gelfand.
Photo by Jack Mitchel.

Cover (bottom photo):
Jennifer Shrewsbury and
Leanne Schreiner.
Photo by Ted Zapel.

Backcover:
Jennifer Shrewsbury and
Jennifer Stone.
Photo by Ted Zapel.

Page vii:
David Howard and Jennifer Gelfand.
Photo by Victor Deliso.

Page 3:
David Howard.
Photo by Victor Deliso.

Page 6:
Kate Goehegan, Ramsey Brown, Gardner
and Abigail von Trapp with Pamela
Whitehill.
Photo by Susan Hoyt von Trapp.

Page 10:
Kate Goehegan, Ramsey Brown, Gardner
and Abigail von Trapp with Pamela
Whitehill. Photo by Susan Hoyt von Trapp.

Page 12:
Megan Jameson and Kristina Weller.
Photo by N. James Whitehill, III.

Page 18:
Esther Geoffery and Jennifer Shrewsbury.
Photo by Ted Zapel.

Page 21:
Jennifer Shrewsbury, Jennifer Stone, and
Leanne Schreiner.
Photo by Ted Zapel.

Page 24:
Ashley and Summer Kircher.
Photo by Ted Zapel.

Page 27:
Christopher Kevlin and Pamela Whitehill.
Photo by J.R. Mosler.

Page 32:
Lauren E. Gelfand.
Photo by Jack Mitchel.

Page 36:
Rebecca Rosenberg, Emily Shanks, Blake
Hazard, Tiffany Vickers.
Photo courtesy of Vermont Conservatory
of Ballet.

Page 39:
Brandon Schreider, Eric Schreider,
Elizabeth Turner, Kristina Weller,
Julianne Lyon.
Photo by Susan Hoyt von Trapp.

Page 46:
Julianne Lyon.
Photo by Susan Hoyt von Trapp

Page 51:
Pamela Whitehill.
Photo by Bertha T. Kourey.

Page 52:
Pamela and Angela Whitehill.
Photo by Dana Jenkins.

Page 60:
Photo by Ted Zapel.

Page 64:
Karl von Rabineau.
Photo by Dana Jenkins.

Page 65:
Pamela Whitehill.
Photo by Jim Abel.

Page 67:
Pamela Whitehill and Frank Dellapolla.
Photo by Ralph J. Carbo, Jr.

Page 68:
Peter Morrison and William Thompson.
Photo by Ralph J. Carbo, Jr.

Page 74:
Tiffany Vickers, Sara Copeland, and
Mariah McNamara.
Berkshire Ballet Company audition.
Photo by N. James Whitehill, III.

Page 77 (top photo):
Brandon Schneider, Mariah McNamara,
Angela Bernard and other aspirants.
Berkshire Ballet Company "Nutcracker"
auditions.
Photo by N. James Whitehill, III.
Page 77 (bottom photo):
Jane Overfield, Norma Gile, Sara Copeland,
and Megan Waite.
Berkshire Ballet Company audition.
Photo by N. James Whitehill, III.
Page 86:
Kate Thorngren.
Photo by Ted Zapel.
Page 92:
Vermont Ballet Theatre dancers in
performance.
Photo by Ralph J. Carbo, Jr.
Page 97:
Dawn Pisor and Kate Thorngren
Photo by Ted Zapel.
Page 100:
Dawn Pisor.
Photo by Art Zapel.
Page 105:
Pamela Whitehill.
Photo by Dana Jenkins.
Page 108:
Pamela Whitehill, Christopher Harris, and
Frank Dellapolla.
Photo by Bertha T. Kourey.
Page 112:
Members of the Mohawk Valley
Performing Arts Company.

Page 116:
Vermont Ballet Theatre.
Photo by Ralph J. Carbo, Jr.
Page 119:
Floyd Flyn.
Photo by Ralph J. Carbo, Jr.
Page 126:
Pamela Whitehill.
Photo by Norman J. Whitehill, Jr.
Page 133:
Kate Thorngren and Dawn Pisor.
Photo by Ted Zapel.
Page 138:
Kate Thorngren and Dawn Pisor.
Photo by Ted Zapel.
Page 146:
Pamela Whitehill and Frank Dellapolla.
Photo by Ralph J. Carbo, Jr.
Page 152:
Julie Stahl and Frank Dellapolla in
LES SYLPHIDES.
Photo by Bertha T. Kourey.
Page 155:
Resumé of Pamela Whitehill.
Photos by Martha Swope.
Page 181:
William P. Noble and
Angela Whitehill.
Photo by N. James Whitehill, III.

Do You Have A Friend That Would Like To Order A Copy Of This Book?

If so, cut out this page for their use. Should they need further information about the book, below is the description as listed in our catalog:

THE PARENTS BOOK OF BALLET
By ANGELA WHITEHILL and WILLIAM NOBLE
A book of answers to critical questions about the care and development of a young dancer.
Though designed as a guidebook for parents, this book about ballet for young dancers is of great interest to the dancers themselves. It provides a glimpse into the entire ballet training process. It tells where to study, whether or when to attend a boarding school, how to find the right teacher and much more. *Divided into seven sections:* (1) The Beginning Years, (2) The Recital Trap, (3) The Pre-Teen Years, (4) Auditions for the Young Dancer, (5) The Early-Teen Years, (6) Summer Programs, and (7) The Later Years. Foreword by international TV, film and stage ballet master, David Howard.   ISBN #0-916260-52-6
Paperback Book: $10.95

—————————ORDER FORM—————————